PERSONAL
DEVELOPMENT
WITH THE
ZODIAC
ORACLE

PERSONAL DEVELOPMENT
WITH THE
ZODIAC
ORACLE

ALAN BUTLER

quantum

LONDON • NEW YORK • TORONTO • SYDNEY

quantum

An imprint of W. Foulsham & Co. Ltd
The Publishing House, Bennetts Close,
Cippenham, Slough, Berkshire, SL1 5AP, England

*This book is dedicated to anyone who is troubled,
perplexed or in need of a friend*

ISBN 0–572–02766-4

Cover illustration by Jurgen Ziewe

Previously published as *Self Development with the Zodiac Oracle*.

Printed in Great Britain by St. Edmundsbury Press, Bury St. Edmunds, Suffolk

Contents

Foreword

he first edition of *Self Development with the Zodiac Oracle* appeared in print ten years ago. For me, the intervening years have been eventful. They have entailed a solid decade of research, specifically into the very earliest interest our ancient ancestors took in the star-clad heavens that ruled their religion and their practical day-to-day lives. I now understand the technicalities underpinning humanity's fascination with astronomy and astrology much better than I did when the Zodiac Oracle was created, and I marvel at the knowledge of people over 4000 years ago who had no written language but whose patience, perseverance and mathematical skills were truly exceptional.

Through my own discoveries in the field of ancient cosmologies, and in my co-operation with other interested researchers, I have gained an ever greater understanding of the absolute importance of the Earth's position as part of the family of planets we know as our solar system. I confidently expect that within the next decade even case-hardened scientists, who have often repudiated the very basis upon which astrology functions, will be forced to acknowledge that even the very structure of our brains is totally dependent on the relationship that the Earth enjoys with its immediate neighbours in space. In other words, astrology – a discipline that predates all other forms of scientific study – will be vindicated.

But at the end of all researches, no matter how much they intrigue us, lies faith, which cannot be validated by numbers on a scientific calculator or bolstered by university doctorates. It was faith that took the Ancient Greeks up the slopes of Delphi to consult the oracles there, who for centuries were revered across the known world. Faith caused devotees to listen carefully to hundreds of generations of shamanic oracles in dozens of cultures, and to act upon the advice they received. This same faith in our own instincts premeditates so many of our actions in a day-to-day sense that we often fail to register that we are employing it. And though scientists may search from now until our great and glorious Sun dulls and reddens, they will never be able adequately to explain what causes us simply to believe. I have seen enough in my half century on the Earth to know that faith and belief genuinely can move mountains.

I remain absolutely convinced that everything we see around us in the natural world is underpinned by forces that we are barely capable of understanding, however much we learn about them. In this I know myself to be in good company, for it is a basic instinct that I share with the vast majority of my brothers and sisters upon this sacred little green globe we inhabit.

If you want to know why the Zodiac Oracle works in the way it does, then perhaps you have failed to understand its primary purpose. Simply follow the procedures outlined in the pages that follow, and look carefully at the advice you are offered. It may not always be easy to understand what the Oracle is trying to tell you, but the ultimate result is generally worth the effort. And though the responses of the Zodiac Oracle might not exactly be in tune with our quick-fix culture, it enjoys an illustrious and truly ancient ancestry.

Alan Butler

Introduction

 ersonal Development with the Zodiac Oracle is a very unusual book. It was created in the first place to offer advice to people who are confused or troubled, but it will also be of use to any individual who is interested in astrology or numerology. The work hinges on one basic premise: that everything on the Earth, material and spiritual, responds to the subtle influences of planetary movement and interaction. This belief has grown into the complex and fascinating subject of astrology, an exacting craft, the origins of which are lost in the mists of time.

Sophisticated astrological systems existed in the Babylonian and ancient Egyptian eras. By early medieval times the practice of astrology had branched into three divisions: judicial astrology, which is the creation of individual horoscopes for interpretation; horary astrology, the art of interpreting a chart cast for a particular moment, pertinent to answering a particular question; and mundane astrology, which forecasts events of national importance.

Many people have had their personal birth charts, or horoscopes, cast by a reputable astrologer, and have discovered for themselves how accurate astrology can be in terms of character analysis, potential future trends and spiritual growth. What very few individuals, surprisingly even devotees of the craft, realise is that the influence of astrology doesn't end with human nature. In reality it was more likely to have been a desire to understand the world about them that encouraged early cultures to take an interest in the star-clad heavens, rather than a desire to discover what lay in store for the individual within the group.

It stands to reason that if every object in the world is ruled by, or perhaps more properly affected by, the stars and planets, there must be an intimate relationship between all such objects and, arguably, a link that exists on a spiritual as well as the more easily understood physical plane. It is this subtle yet inextricable association between the component parts that make up creation which is utilised in the divination procedure and responses of the Zodiac Oracle.

The reader will discover in the next section how to obtain a response from the Zodiac Oracle, but individuals who are not serious adherents of astrology may well still be puzzled as to why the book works in the way that it does. The short answer is that the Oracle works because the enquirer has a need that it should do so; in fact experience has proved that the greater the requirement of the user, the more sympathetic and accurate the response is likely to be.

To many this will be no satisfactory answer, yet oracles of all kinds have been consulted by humankind since time immemorial and have never diminished in popularity.

We might find a partial rationale for the validity of oracles in the theory of synchronicity, a word first coined by the famous psychologist Carl Jung, who was a contemporary and originally a pupil of Sigmund Freud. Jung speculated that there are inextricable links between all events, and the effects of a tiny minority of these we observe as apparent coincidences. Often such happenings string themselves together, forming the most complex and astounding patterns. These constitute the tip of a fantastic iceberg that appears in the conscious world but is in fact only a tiny part of the synchronicity that we might observe on a subconscious level. It might be argued that a book such as *Personal Development with the Zodiac Oracle* only puts us in touch with what we already know well, though on a subconscious level. Whatever the answer may be, there are hundreds of testimonies to the ways in which this work has assisted people to discover more about themselves and the workings of their innermost minds.

It must be stated from the outset that the Zodiac Oracle will not work for everyone immediately, and again there is no definitive explanation for why this is so. Some readers will find an affinity with its format and purpose at once, whilst for others it will take time and practice to understand what message the Zodiac Oracle is seeking to impart. One fact is certain however. No person who is genuinely open-minded or in need of a friend will be disappointed.

About the
Zodiac Oracle

he Zodiac Oracle is composed of 360 responses. These are short stories, or fables, and have been carefully constructed in such a way that each of them responds to a specific degree of the zodiac wheel.

At the beginning of the book you will find outlined the procedure for divination. Readers will be able to consult the Oracle about any question or problem that may be on their mind. The divination procedure is based on Cabbalistic numerology and has been specifically designed so that – through a series of simple conversion tables – the name of the questioner and the time and date of the enquiry will lead to a particular sign and degree of the zodiac. The Oracle will not necessarily provide the answer that the reader expects but the one that is most relevant to the question. The Oracle's responses come in the form of short stories, observations or parables – a method of offering advice that has been common to oracles the world over. Some short meditation on the response may initially be necessary, though the Oracle often works with such startling clarity that the questioner is left in no doubt as to the meaning and significance of the response.

When turning to the relevant zodiac sign, the reader will first come across a short passage related to the characteristics of that segment of the zodiac. This forms the first part of the Oracle's response. When the sign degree is consulted, the prime response is a short story or statement, this being the second and major part of the Oracle's response to any given enquiry.

Several words follow the degree response.

The first is the Keyword. This single word may be useful as a quick reference to the Oracle's response to any given question, though the reader must understand that for a holistic and accurate understanding of the Zodiac Oracle's response, the various passages should be read and considered in full and carefully.

Second is the element, which indicates the elemental rulership of the sign in question, for example fire. Explanations of the four elements can be found at the back of the Oracle (see pages 151–54). Some readers may find these useful when interpreting responses.

Finally there is the planet – that associated in classical astrology with the sign in question, for example Mars. At the back of the book is an explanation of the planets and their functions in astrological rulership (see pages 141–49). The reader may find that this explanation is also helpful in answering the original enquiry.

The Zodiac Oracle

sing the system of Cabbalistic numerology necessary to consult the Oracle is very simple. All you need is a pen and a piece of paper. Almost any sort of question is relevant, provided it is asked with a genuine need, though the responses that you receive may sometimes surprise you and could even answer a more fundamental question than the one you originally asked.

First of all it is very important to visualise inwardly the question or problem that is uppermost in your mind. Keep the enquiry as simple as possible because if you visualise a compound question the responses you receive might not be too easy to understand.

See if you can find a quiet spot in which to consult the Oracle, away from noise or possible interruptions. If there are too many distractions your concentration will be affected, making it difficult for you to hold the visualisation in your mind. Once you have meditated for a moment or two on your question or problem, take the pen and paper and write your name down the left-hand column as shown below. Use the name that you are usually known by if it is different from your full name. Below is an example name and the way that you should list it on the paper.

J
O
H
N

S
M
I
T
H

Now turn to Table A on page 17. Here you will find a list of phonetic sounds and their corresponding Cabbalistic number values. Becoming accustomed to using the phonetic table will take a short while but you will soon find it quite easy. Take the sounds of your name, break them down into phonetic components and write the corresponding number value against the letter, or group of letters, in question.

For example, J is in the line I – Y – J – Ee and has a number value of 10, so against J write down the number 10.

$$J = 10$$

The sound O has a value of 16, so write that down beside the letter O in John.

$$O = 16$$

In the name John, the letter H is not sounded so we miss it out.

The next letter, N, is valued at 14, and this is the number to jot down beside it. Continue in this way until you have completed the name.

$$
\begin{aligned}
J &= 10 \\
O &= 16 \\
H &= 0 \\
N &= 14 \\[6pt]
S &= 21 \\
M &= 13 \\
I &= 10 \\
TH &= 9
\end{aligned}
$$

To the bottom of this list you now need to add the time you are asking the question, breaking this down into hours and minutes and using the 12-hour clock. If, in our example, the question was asked at half past ten in the evening, the list would look as follows:

$$J = 10$$
$$O = 16$$
$$H = 0$$
$$N = 14$$

$$S = 21$$
$$M = 13$$
$$I = 10$$
$$TH = 9$$
$$10$$
$$30$$

Now add all the numbers together. In the example the resultant figure is 133.

Now turn to Table B on page 18 and find your number in one of the right-hand columns. Trace back to the left in the same column until you arrive at the name of a zodiac sign. This is the sign that your answer lies in. In the example, the sign would be Pisces.

To obtain the degree of the sign that forms the answer to your question, you need to follow a similar procedure but this time use the date on which the question is asked instead of your name. Let us say, for example, that the question was asked on 3 October 2002. You would then add the following numbers to the list.

3
10
2
0
0
2

Finally, you need to add the time. The clock will usually have moved on a minute or two while you were carrying out your original calculations so in the example we will assume that the time is now 32 minutes past ten. The list now looks like this:

3
10
2
0
0
2
10
32

Once again add the numbers together, and this time refer for your answer to Table C on page 19. Find your number in the right-hand columns and then trace across to the left side to discover the degree of the sign that contains the response relating to your enquiry. The example adds up to 59 and so the degree of Pisces where the relevant advice can be found will be 15 degrees.

You now have several responses to read. The first is the Zodiac sign description. This will often reflect the attitude that you take towards your enquiry. Next comes the main response – the short story occupying the Zodiac degree that you have arrived at. This should be the solution or advice that you are seeking, though remember it may take some thought before you respond fully to its significance. For further verification you can look at the Keyword, and also the element ruler and planet ruler, mentioned in the previous section.

A word of caution. The Zodiac Oracle was never meant to be a party game, and in its own gentle way it may rebuke you if you use it as such. Concentration on your real problems and a reverence for the timeless methods that the Oracle uses should lead you to the answers you need, though not necessarily the ones you expected. Use the Oracle with care and it will not let you down.

TABLE A

NUMBER	SOUND
1	A-Ah-Aa
2	B
3	G
4	D
5	E-Eh-Ay
6	U-V-W-O-o
7	Z
8	H-Ch
9	Th
10	I-Y-J-Ee
11	C-K-Ck
12	L
13	M
14	N
15	X
16	O-Oh
17	F-P-Ph
18	Sh-Ts-Tz
19	Q
20	R
21	S
22	T

TABLE B

Sign																														
Aries	1	24	25	48	49	72	73	96	97	120	121	144	145	168	169	192	193	216	217	240	241	264	265	288	289	312	313	336	337	360
Taurus	2	23	26	47	50	71	74	95	98	119	122	143	146	167	170	191	194	215	218	239	242	263	266	287	290	311	314	335	338	359
Gemini	3	22	27	46	51	70	75	94	99	118	123	142	147	166	171	190	195	214	219	238	243	262	267	286	291	310	315	334	339	358
Cancer	4	21	28	45	52	69	76	93	100	117	124	141	148	165	172	189	196	213	220	237	244	261	268	285	292	309	316	333	340	357
Leo	5	20	29	44	53	68	77	92	101	116	125	140	149	164	173	188	197	212	221	236	245	260	269	284	293	308	317	332	341	356
Virgo	6	19	30	43	54	67	78	91	102	115	126	139	150	163	174	187	198	211	222	235	246	259	270	283	294	307	318	331	342	355
Libra	7	18	31	42	55	66	79	90	103	114	127	138	151	162	175	186	199	210	223	234	247	258	271	282	295	306	319	330	343	354
Scorpio	8	17	32	41	56	65	80	89	104	113	128	137	152	161	176	185	200	209	224	233	248	257	272	281	296	305	320	329	344	353
Sagittarius	9	16	33	40	57	64	81	88	105	112	129	136	153	160	177	184	201	208	225	232	249	256	273	280	297	304	321	328	345	352
Capricorn	10	15	34	39	58	63	82	87	106	111	130	135	154	159	178	183	202	207	226	231	250	255	274	279	298	303	322	327	346	351
Aquarius	11	14	35	38	59	62	83	86	107	110	131	134	155	158	179	182	203	206	227	230	251	254	275	278	299	302	323	326	347	350
Pisces	12	13	36	37	60	61	84	85	108	109	132	133	156	157	180	181	204	205	228	229	252	253	276	277	300	301	324	325	348	349

TABLE C

1°	29	31	89	91	149	151	209	211	269	271	329	331
2°	27	33	87	93	147	153	207	213	267	273	327	333
3°	25	35	85	95	145	155	205	215	265	275	325	335
4°	23	37	83	97	143	157	203	217	263	277	323	337
5°	21	39	81	99	141	159	201	219	261	279	321	339
6°	19	41	79	101	139	161	199	221	259	281	319	341
7°	17	43	77	103	137	163	197	223	257	283	317	343
8°	15	45	75	105	135	165	195	225	255	285	315	345
9°	13	47	73	107	133	167	193	227	253	287	313	347
10°	11	49	71	109	131	169	191	229	251	289	311	349
11°	9	51	69	111	129	171	189	231	249	291	309	351
12°	7	53	67	113	127	173	187	233	247	293	307	353
13°	5	55	65	115	125	175	185	235	245	295	305	355
14°	3	57	63	117	123	177	183	237	243	297	303	357
15°	1	59	61	119	121	179	181	239	241	299	301	359
16°	2	60	62	120	122	180	182	240	242	300	302	360
17°	4	58	64	118	124	178	184	238	244	298	304	358
18°	6	56	66	116	126	176	186	236	246	296	306	356
19°	8	54	68	114	128	174	188	234	248	294	308	354
20°	10	52	70	112	130	172	190	232	250	292	310	352
21°	12	50	72	110	132	170	192	230	252	290	312	350
22°	14	48	74	108	134	168	194	228	254	288	314	348
23°	16	46	76	106	136	166	196	226	256	286	316	346
24°	18	44	78	104	138	164	198	224	258	284	308	344
25°	20	42	80	102	140	162	200	222	260	282	320	342
26°	22	40	82	100	142	160	202	220	262	280	322	340
27°	24	38	84	98	144	158	204	218	264	278	324	338
28°	26	36	86	96	146	156	206	216	266	276	326	336
29°	28	34	88	94	148	154	208	214	268	274	328	334
30°	30	32	90	92	150	152	210	212	270	272	330	332

ARIES

♈

Out of the chaos comes order.
In the midst of the void a pattern is
discernible. Within this pattern,
consciousness is born and the spring of
human spiritual endeavour can flow
around the Earth and out into the
boundless universe beyond.

Moon	Sun	Mercury	Venus	Mars
☽	☉	☿	♀	♂
Jupiter	Saturn	Uranus	Neptune	Pluto
♃	♄	♅	♆	♇

DEGREE 1

The machine-gun's rattle is at last silent and in the squalor and filth of the trench the soldier has time to write a letter. In it he talks of the joys of summer and the warmth of a remembered embrace. Meanwhile, the rats scamper unconcerned around his feet in the mud.

Keyword
Respite

Element
Fire

Planet
Mars ♂

DEGREE 2

Keyword
Compassion

Element
Fire

Planet
Mars ♂

Although he is employed to prevent theft, for two years the store detective has watched a particularly frail old lady deposit a small packet of tea into her shopping bag on the same day each week. Feeling himself powerless to prevent this occurrence, the detective is ruthless in his vigilance on every other occasion.

DEGREE 3

The arrival of the lamb is perhaps the first true herald of spring. On what seems like the coldest of days, when a frost still clings to the grass and snow lies heavy on the hills, the new lambs are there, a certain sign that the first flowers of nature's revival will soon bedeck the hedgerows.

Keyword
Hope

Element
Fire

Planet
Mars ♂

DEGREE 4

Keyword
Originality

Element
Fire

Planet
Mars ♂

The smithy is warm and the bellows busy as the burly blacksmith works with his hammer and hot iron at the anvil. The horseshoe that he is creating is identical to, though uniquely different from, every other that he has manufactured in his long career. The blacksmith knows this, though his apprentice, who pumps the bellows, is bored with the monotony of his routine.

DEGREE 5

A certain old countryman is proud of his ability to trap the rabbits in his district. Because of his skill and experience no other local can better his exploits. Late one spring the countryman walks to his allotment, intent on picking succulent spring greens for his dinner. Upon arriving at the plot, he discovers that his entire crop has been eaten by rabbits.

Keyword
Return

Element
Fire

Planet
Mars ♂

DEGREE 6

Keyword
Observation

Element
Fire

Planet
Mars ♂

Rooks are notorious for being ragged and untidy birds, and are often regarded as thieves. Though they are intelligent, their numbers have been kept low by farmers whose first aim is to protect their crops. For centuries, however, experienced folklorists have gauged the heat of the coming summer by noting at what height in the trees the rooks build their nests.

DEGREE 7

Filled with aggression, an angry child smashes her toys in a frenzy of frustration. She is not aware that her future pleasure may be marred by her present state, for in the depths of anger or sorrow there is no tomorrow. Later the aggression will be forgotten but the toys will still be broken.

Keyword
Far-sightedness

Element
Fire

Planet
Mars ♂

DEGREE 8

Keyword
Control

Element
Fire

Planet
Mars ♂

Speaking in purely human terms, hyenas are a cowardly species. Waiting on the periphery of a kill until the lion or other predator wanders off, they then dash in to salvage the remnants. Despite their apparent cowardice, however, hyenas possess jaws capable of smashing the largest of bones as if they were matches.

DEGREE 9

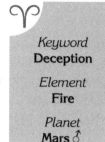

At the end of a busy and fairly lucrative day, the onion seller prepares to return to his home for a well earned rest. Before doing so he visits a gentlemen's cloakroom in the town to change his clothes. When he emerges, his beret and French accent have mysteriously disappeared and now, like most of his neighbours, he carries an umbrella and a briefcase.

Keyword
Deception

Element
Fire

Planet
Mars ♂

DEGREE 10

Keyword
Underestimation

Element
Fire

Planet
Mars ♂

Few people notice the elderly businessman who throws bread to the wildfowl on the park lake. To most passers-by he is a nondescript character who has no tangible effect on their lives. Three or four generations of birds, however, have viewed him as god and provider, for winter and summer alike he is always there. On one level he is invisible whilst on another he is revered.

DEGREE 11

The workers stoking a greedy furnace are parched by the searing heat. As they sweat at their toil, above in the bath house a merchant, seeking relief from the pressures of the day, sits and perspires in happy relaxation in the steam room that the furnace supplies with heat.

Keyword
Degree

Element
Fire

Planet
Sun ☉

DEGREE 12

Keyword
Alternatives

Element
Fire

Planet
Sun ☉

Before the returning soldier the long road stretches ahead. Such a distance would have seemed much shorter with victory to spur him on but in the face of defeat he is feeling every mile. Hanging dead on the barbed wire back at the battlefield is another soldier whose army was victorious.

DEGREE 13

The planet Mars is a cold and inhospitable world with a thin and poisonous atmosphere and little of apparent benefit when viewed in comparison with our own planet. It may, however, be rich in precious minerals, and the sight of red Mars, when viewed from the Earth, is one of the most beautiful spectacles in the sky.

Keyword
Obscuration

Element
Fire

Planet
Sun ☉

DEGREE 14

Keyword
Compassion

Element
Fire

Planet
Sun ☉

At the moment that his opponent is wavering slightly and obviously groggy, the prize fighter fails to attack as strongly as he should and as a result subsequently loses the contest. When questioned later as to why he hesitated, the seasoned pugilist replies that he sensed that his opponent tonight could not stand the humiliation of defeat.

DEGREE 15

In the witness box in a courtroom a woman defends her lover, who is the accused. She declares him incapable of the brutality with which he is charged. Although she is aware that she is committing perjury, the woman is equally certain that the statement she is making is true, at least from her own experience.

Keyword
Blindness

Element
Fire

Planet
Sun ☉

DEGREE 16

Keyword
Recognition

Element
Fire

Planet
Sun ☉

High above the valley a ram stands on a rocky outcrop surveying the flock close by. In his horns he has had sufficient power to fight his way to the top of the pecking order and he still has tenacity enough to maintain his position. When he is confronted by potentially harmless mountaineers, despite his strength and endurance he flees to safety, together with the rest of his herd, weak and strong alike.

DEGREE 17

Whilst plundering a house a certain burglar is disturbed by the occupant, who is armed with a shotgun. The thief does not put up a struggle and is delivered into the hands of the police. In the end not only is the burglar arrested but also the house owner, for possessing a shotgun without a licence.

Keyword
Apportioning

Element
Fire

Planet
Sun ☉

DEGREE 18

Keyword
Observation

Element
Fire

Planet
Sun ☉

Intent upon a well-tried line of patter, the door-to-door vacuum cleaner salesman spends 20 minutes extolling the virtues of his product to a housewife. She tries to explain to him that she has no need of his machine but he carries on. Eventually she invites him into her house, where he sees that there are no electric power points to run the machine from.

DEGREE 19

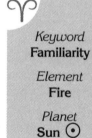

Expertly the fire eater transfers a flame from a fiery brand to his mouth and back to the brand again. Those in the audience marvel at his skill and ability to manipulate so dangerous a medium. One night the performer returns home after the show to find that during his absence a fire has broken out and burned his house down.

Keyword
Familiarity

Element
Fire

Planet
Sun ☉

DEGREE 20

Keyword
Fickle

Element
Fire

Planet
Sun ☉

On a street corner a young woman stands collecting information for an advertising company promoting a new product. After a while she notices that the general reaction to the merchandise is not favourable, though many people admit to using it. A year later the opinions of most people are no more favourable, although the product is still selling well.

DEGREE 21

An apprentice tries hard to copy a complex joint being cut by the master carpenter. After much perseverance, he manages to replicate the joint, though it is ill fitting and misshapen. The carpenter explains that when the apprentice starts to visualise the chair that he is making, the joint itself will become easy to create.

Keyword
Holism

Element
Fire

Planet
Jupiter ♃

DEGREE 22

Keyword
Adaptability

Element
Fire

Planet
Jupiter ♃

In spite of its tremendous size and seemingly awkward gait, a bear rarely goes hungry and is skilled in many different techniques for satisfying its appetite. Although it can survive alone in a harsh world it is not beyond plundering easy pickings if they lie within its reach. The bear will even steal from the habitation of man, its only natural enemy, if circumstances allow.

DEGREE 23

An elderly and bedraggled lady is arrested for vagrancy because she is caught scavenging in a dustbin. When she receives only a caution she is flabbergasted. Questioned afterwards as to why she was surprised at the verdict, she explains that she expected to go to prison because the dustbin was that of a wealthy family.

Keyword
Perspective

Element
Fire

Planet
Jupiter ♃

DEGREE 24

Keyword
Flexibility

Element
Fire

Planet
Jupiter ♃

In legend the wolf stands alone as the archetypal villain and pack hunter. He has been maligned and chased out of many countries where the species once flourished. The wolf's value ecologically is in culling sick and old animals from large herds, thereby keeping the strain pure, though for all his skills at hunting over vast distances and his awesome reputation, a great percentage of the average wolf's diet is humble mice.

DEGREE 25

Arriving at a building site one day a contractor discovers that vandals have wrecked some of his equipment during the night. Because of this eventuality he is forced to lay off some of his workers temporarily. One of the labourers returns home unaware that amongst the vandals was his own son.

Keyword
Repercussions

Element
Fire

Planet
Jupiter ♃

DEGREE 26

Keyword
Patience

Element
Fire

Planet
Jupiter ♃

High on a lofty perch the regal and patient eagle surveys the countryside below. Barely a creature moves, no matter how small or distant, that is not observed by the eagle perched above. Each grass snake and vole is seen through the long hours of silent vigilance, though only rarely does the great bird leave its perch to dive for food. When it does so it is invariably successful.

DEGREE 27

A case of rifles is captured by a tribe of bushmen, but never having seen such devices before, they know of the power of the guns only through folk tales. They know the objects to have powerful magic but after trying the rifles as clubs and cudgels, breaking several in the attempt, they contemptuously throw them away and return to their accustomed spears.

Keyword
Ignorance

Element
Fire

Planet
Jupiter ♃

DEGREE 28

Keyword
Concentration

Element
Fire

Planet
Jupiter ♃

A certain car salesman is expert at selling the model of car for which he is responsible, having memorised all its technical specifications and being in any case a naturally good talker. Prospective customers cannot see the salesman's own car at the rear of the building, a different model altogether.

DEGREE 29

Two people argue. The basis of their disagreement is that a bus has just passed with only one seat available and both individuals claim to have been first in the queue. Whilst they stand and bandy words three almost empty buses come and go.

Keyword
Obstinacy

Element
Fire

Planet
Jupiter ♃

DEGREE 30

Keyword
Gratitude

Element
Fire

Planet
Jupiter ♃

When a competition winner discovers that the prize to which he is entitled is inferior to that which has been promised he is furious. In his anger he fails to realise that only a few hours previously he never even seriously considered the possibility of winning.

ZODIAC SIGN 2
TAURUS
♉

A mighty river flows between the known and the unknown. Some say the ferryman demands a fee. But every journey must commence, and to those who genuinely trust, the cost is an irrelevant detail. If the quest is imperative there will be no significant obstacles.

Moon	Sun	Mercury	Venus	Mars
☽	☉	☿	♀	♂
Jupiter	Saturn	Uranus	Neptune	Pluto
♃	♄	♅	♆	♇

DEGREE 1

As the talented artist deftly puts the finishing touches to his latest portrait he scrutinises the canvas and then stares at the attractive model who has been sitting for him. Without a sigh or any sign of frustration the artist destroys the canvas and dismisses his model. She is perplexed but satisfied enough that she has been paid. The artist considers the money well spent.

Keyword
Continuation

Element
Earth

Planet
Venus ♀

DEGREE 2

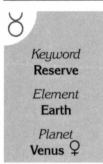

Keyword
Reserve

Element
Earth

Planet
Venus ♀

If treated gently and in a favourable mood, an often wild and ferocious bull can be led around by the farm children. However, should the bull be ill-used or prevented from following his chosen path, the strongest farmhands have difficulty in controlling him.

DEGREE 3

Paying their entrance fee, the queue of men quickly pass through the turnstile and on into the strip club in the red-light district. Amongst the group are individuals who have been coerced by their companions into visiting the spectacle. Their reaction may well be one of boredom or revulsion, but would they admit it?

Keyword
Acquiescence

Element
Earth

Planet
Venus ♀

DEGREE 4

Keyword
Evolution

Element
Earth

Planet
Venus ♀

There is no permanence to the artistic creations that a hairdresser is responsible for making, no matter how talented the person concerned. The natural processes of hair growth are certain to win through in the end and then the client will be forced to return to the hairdresser once more for a temporary suspension of a time-ruled event.

DEGREE 5

A gardener working for a large estate views with satisfaction the fresh new blooms of spring that, thanks to his constant care and attention, grow in neat order in the garden. Beyond the perimeters of the gardener's kingdom, in the tangle of vegetation at the far side of the wall, the colours are just as bright, the scent as strong and the number of species greater.

Keyword
Endeavour

Element
Earth

Planet
Venus ♀

DEGREE 6

Keyword
Resilience

Element
Earth

Planet
Venus ♀

During the early 1950s, the rabbit population of Western Europe was virtually decimated by myxomatosis, introduced to control the rabbits' numbers. Despite this scourge, such is the resilience of the species that it has now recovered and, much to the alarm of farmers, is breeding as prolifically as ever.

DEGREE 7

Members of a world-famous orchestra are touring in a foreign country. One day a number of instruments are stolen whilst in transit. A double bass player, who has always been teased because of his bulky and awkward instrument, is relieved to find that his bass was too large for the thieves to tackle, though smaller instruments of greater value may never be recovered.

Keyword
Eventuality

Element
Earth

Planet
Venus ♀

DEGREE 8

Keyword
Inspiration

Element
Earth

Planet
Venus ♀

A poet who has recently visited a place of outstanding natural beauty completes a work dedicated to his personal appreciation of the scene. Future readers of the work may never have the chance to stand where the poet himself did, but in any geographical location can relive the creator's emotions.

DEGREE 9

A vegetable stall in a busy market is surrounded by eager shoppers, but the stall holder is delaying business bargaining with a passer-by. Eventually, bored with the conversation, the time-waster saunters off. The stall holder prepares to serve the next customer but finds that the queue has diminished because many of his customers have grown tired of waiting.

Keyword
Procrastination

Element
Earth

Planet
Venus ♀

Keyword
Simplicity

Element
Earth

Planet
Venus ♀

DEGREE 10

The maypole is freshly painted and has brightly coloured ribbons hanging from the top. Groups of children dance round the pole, weaving the ribbons into an intricate pattern. Historians recognise the symbolism and heritage of the maypole; the children merely find the dances an amusing diversion.

DEGREE 11

Whilst his neighbours are busy chopping wood for the winter, a popular though idle homesteader talks away the hot summer hours, leaving himself with little fuel laid up. Such is the nature of the man, lazy or not, that with the winter he tours the houses of his friends where he is made welcome and is able to share the warmth of their fires.

Keyword
Resource

Element
Earth

Planet
Mercury ☿

Keyword
Regret

Element
Earth

Planet
Mercury ☿

DEGREE 12

In a smart plush office a bank manager sits pensive. He has just refused a loan to a failing businessman who has dejectedly left the premises. Although the bank manager had the power to grant the loan, he did not wish to perpetuate stress and suffering by doing so. Still he cannot avoid feeling himself a traitor.

DEGREE 13

The rhinoceros has the build and destructive ability of a tank. Its sheer bulk and uncertain temper have kept it safe from predators for countless millennia. Like so many other creatures it is not immune to bullets, and for nothing more important than its short fibrous horn it has been hunted to the brink of extinction. Being so large it is easy to track and kill.

Keyword
Dimension

Element
Earth

Planet
Mercury ☿

DEGREE 14

Keyword
Tolerance

Element
Earth

Planet
Mercury ☿

With little else to do all day but keep her house meticulously clean, the wife of a prosperous businessman takes a great pride in her home. Such is the obsessive nature of the woman that she even tidies around visitors who drop crumbs or spill cigarette ash. All too soon she has no one but herself to appreciate the pristine house.

DEGREE 15

Spending hours in preparation, bathing and adorning herself, a young woman is certain that this procedure makes her more attractive and alluring. Her friend, a bright and happy person, but one who is less meticulous about her appearance, is never short of friends and has more time to appreciate them.

Keyword
Moderation

Element
Earth

Planet
Mercury ☿

DEGREE 16

Keyword
Appreciation

Element
Earth

Planet
Mercury ☿

An old tailor sits with needle in hand, marvelling at the quality of the cloth he is presently engaged upon. He observes and appreciates the beauty in the weave, recognising not only the mill but also the very machine that manufactured the cloth. The tailor is by no means a rich man but would gladly make up this suit for nothing if it were necessary.

DEGREE 17

Working long hard hours ,the farmer constantly keeps an eye on the weather, which can thwart all his efforts at a single stroke. He would not change his lifestyle despite his worries, but neither can he alter the climate.

Keyword
Limitations

Element
Earth

Planet
Mercury ☿

DEGREE 18

Keyword
Trepidation

Element
Earth

Planet
Mercury ☿

After weeks of practice, singers in a West End show about to open feel they have never performed more miserably. Despite their best efforts nothing is going right. When opening night arrives, the performance is flawless and well received.

DEGREE 19

In any Christian church the altar, with its crucifix and adornments, is the focal point of worship. Though the congregation face in this direction and are attentive to the ministrations of the priest, most of those attending realise that God's presence is not restricted to this one small area.

Keyword
Realisation

Element
Earth

Planet
Mercury ☿

DEGREE 20

Keyword
Now

Element
Earth

Planet
Mercury ☿

Watching only from a distance, an unsure and shy young man admires an attractive and vivacious woman. The same situation continues for some months until eventually the young woman is married. It is not until years later that the admirer learns from a third party that the object of his affection would have welcomed his advances at the time.

DEGREE 21

The ruling princess of a certain kingdom is faced with the necessity of marriage, primarily to produce an heir. The husband she chooses must be content to remain a consort all his life and will always live in the shadow of his wife. The possible choices for the princess are very few.

♉

Keyword
Dilemma

Element
Earth

Planet
Saturn ♄

♉

Keyword
Observation

Element
Earth

Planet
Saturn ♄

DEGREE 22

Loud applause greets a famous actor who walks out on stage to open in a new play. So bright are the lights that he cannot see the audience, yet because of the noise he knows they are present. The actor plays his part to the disembodied sounds. Since few members of the audience know him personally the actor too is an illusion as far as they are concerned.

DEGREE 23

Left with a roll of cloth that has proved not to be popular, a draper considers how best to dispose of it without losing money. Eventually he cuts it into small pieces and places it amongst a box of remnants, at an apparently cheap price. Now offered in a form that appears to be a bargain the material is quite quickly sold.

♉

Keyword
Ingenuity

Element
Earth

Planet
Saturn ♄

♉

Keyword
Options

Element
Earth

Planet
Saturn ♄

DEGREE 24

Returning from a long journey, a father brings his child an expensive present packed in a large cardboard box. After looking at the gift for a short time the child spends several hours playing with the box.

DEGREE 25

In a remote country hamlet most villagers are pleased to welcome the van salesman who saves them long and tedious trips into town by visiting them each week with his groceries. The local farms send their produce to the cities – the same merchandise with which, in one form or another, the van salesman returns.

Keyword
Puzzle

Element
Earth

Planet
Saturn ♄

DEGREE 26

Keyword
Alternatives

Element
Earth

Planet
Saturn ♄

Popular because of his prompt deliveries, a town milkman thrives and becomes prosperous. Having built his round personally, he finds it easy to maintain. The work is healthy and pleasant. Another milkman in the same town, working for a large combine, views his work as being laborious, cold and poorly paid considering the effort involved.

DEGREE 27

Because of recent over-exertion the feet of a ballet dancer are blistered and sore, as a result of which she is advised not to dance for some time. Such is the power of the music as she waits in the wings undecided before the next performance that she carries on with her programme and feels no pain.

Keyword
Compulsion

Element
Earth

Planet
Saturn ♄

DEGREE 28

Keyword
Absence

Element
Earth

Planet
Saturn ♄

The screams of delight and excitement can be heard all around the fairground as children and adults alike enjoy the thrills offered by the many rides and side-shows. The owner of the fairground sits in his plush and stylish caravan, busy with his accounts, deaf to the pleasure that, in his need to earn a living, he has created.

DEGREE 29

The noise and clamour of a bottling plant in a dairy is a far cry from the peaceful country meadows where cows graze to produce the milk. If milk were green, perhaps those who drink it would better appreciate the sunshine and rain that feed us today, as they always have.

Keyword
Comprehension

Element
Earth

Planet
Saturn ♄

Keyword
Deception

Element
Earth

Planet
Saturn ♄

DEGREE 30

Being successful at apprehending poachers, the gamekeeper has a reputation for efficiency. His employer is duly grateful and increases the keeper's salary. Reflecting upon this, the gamekeeper smiles to himself later as he loads an illicitly won salmon into his car. He will take it 15 miles to a town where he can sell it to a hotelier who is not choosy as to its origin.

GEMINI

♊

What is this peace for which we seek?

Have we stopped to question without

the incessant need for discussions? A

choice must be made between the two,

war or music. Look into the depths of

fathomless space, listen with the ear of

your soul and surely you must hear,

beyond the clamour of silence, the

music of the spheres.

Moon	Sun	Mercury	Venus	Mars
☽	☉	☿	♀	♂
Jupiter	Saturn	Uranus	Neptune	Pluto
♃	♄	♅	♆	♇

DEGREE 1

A student training to be a deep-sea diver cheats by copying the answers from a colleague's paper during an examination. Months later, whilst diving to repair an underwater installation, the individual encounters a faulty oxygen valve and in rising to the surface too quickly suffers unnecessary physical problems.

Keyword
Vision

Element
Air

Planet
Mercury ☿

DEGREE 2

Keyword
Self-deception

Element
Air

Planet
Mercury ☿

An artist creates masterpieces of a superb quality in the style of old masters, passing them off as genuine. Such is his talent that even experienced art critics are fooled. The paintings sell well, though the artist has a studio full of his own work that nobody wishes to buy.

DEGREE 3

Two students are asked, during a lecture, to speak for five minutes each on a subject which is totally alien to their personal experience. One rambles on aimlessly for the full time allowed, whilst the other declines to talk, on the grounds that he fails to relate to the subject. The persistent gabbler receives no marks whilst the individual who said nothing is marked highly.

Keyword
Recognition

Element
Air

Planet
Mercury ☿

DEGREE 4

Keyword
Realisation

Element
Air

Planet
Mercury ☿

During a lecture on handwriting, a graphologist is offered a specimen of script to analyse. She is busily telling the audience about the psychological problems of the individual concerned, stressing the need for concentration and effort on the part of the sample writer, when she suddenly realises that the piece of script was written by herself.

DEGREE 5

In a large and populous kingdom, the monarch constantly keeps his jester in attendance for, or so the courtiers think, his amusement and diversion. When the monarch's advisers disagree or are party to treachery and intrigue, the ruler relies on the unbiased and honest advice of his fool for many of the day-to-day decisions that will affect millions of people.

♊

Keyword
Alternatives

Element
Air

Planet
Mercury ☿

DEGREE 6

♊

Keyword
Visionless

Element
Air

Planet
Mercury ☿

A journalist working for a local newspaper is intent on getting a story from a local councillor. His editor has impressed upon him the importance of the task to such an extent that although the journalist passes the scene of a bank robbery, worthy of national news coverage, he continues on his journey to the town hall.

DEGREE 7

In a rural village, a particular young man is classified as being an imbecile. Not trusted with responsibilities he idles away his time in play and amusement. When a plague strikes the community a great percentage of the population succumbs. The imbecile does not understand the implications of the pestilence and miraculously survives.

Keyword
Nonconformity

Element
Air

Planet
Mercury ☿

DEGREE 8

Keyword
Subterfuge

Element
Air

Planet
Mercury ☿

Asked to act as an intermediary in a border dispute, a diplomat is uncertain how to bridge the gap between the two sides. Although he is aware that arms and supplies are running low for both protagonists, he tells each faction how strong and powerful its opponent is. Soon a peace treaty is signed.

DEGREE 9

In dramatic tones and deliberately embroidering the plot, the story teller speaks of a battle fought many years previously. A simple and unpretentious old man sits in the crowd of attentive listeners. He is a veteran of the battle being spoken of, but though he enjoys listening to the narrative he does not recognise the event that the story teller relates.

Keyword
Time

Element
Air

Planet
Mercury ☿

DEGREE 10

Keyword
Consideration

Element
Air

Planet
Mercury ☿

Supposedly one of our closest relatives in the animal kingdom, the gorilla is a gentle giant, never displaying its great strength unless forced into a situation where this is unavoidable. Even male gorillas are protective of their young. Though ranging far to find the vegetable diet they relish, gorillas will never destroy an area beyond its ability to recover.

DEGREE 11

For many years, thousands of satisfied patients frequented the premises of an apparently qualified physician. Known in the district as something of a miracle worker, he is one day exposed as being a fraud and a quack. Despite his past success, he is no longer visited by his patients.

Keyword
Belief

Element
Air

Planet
Venus ♀

DEGREE 12

Keyword
Evasion

Element
Air

Planet
Venus ♀

For many years a shoplifter is successful in evading detection, such is her ability as a thief. Eventually, despite her best endeavours, she is seen and apprehended. Appearing in court she admits only to the particular offence that she has been charged with, despite the fact that the very clothes she is wearing were stolen from the same store at an earlier date.

DEGREE 13

One could be forgiven for believing on first impression that a talented parrot must have the highest intelligence rating amongst birds. He does not merely speak individual words but is capable of reciting whole passages. Alas, speech without comprehension does not represent intelligence, for the parrot merely mimics and has no understanding of what he says.

Keyword
Deceit

Element
Air

Planet
Venus ♀

Keyword
Persuasion

Element
Air

Planet
Venus ♀

DEGREE 14

Two men must undertake the same journey on a hazardous road to deliver messages. One of the individuals, because of his superior persuasive ability, manages to convince the other that there is little point in them both risking a dangerous undertaking and induces his less quick-witted friend to take his message for him.

DEGREE 15

Ants appear to be individual entities, for each has a body and movement unique to itself. A closer study, however, reveals that each ant is only an extension of the whole colony, for any reasoning and planning ability is possessed only by the ant colony as a whole. The ants' nest could therefore be considered to be one life form.

Keyword
Co-operation

Element
Air

Planet
Venus ♀

Keyword
Inspiration

Element
Air

Planet
Venus ♀

DEGREE 16

An errand boy must make several trips in the same district but has to keep returning to the shop to reload his bicycle. After a little thought he loads all of the merchandise at once onto a handcart. Although the journey takes longer than one trip on the bicycle, overall he saves a great deal of effort and time.

DEGREE 17

Reading a historical diary is a person whose knowledge of the calendar is limited. He notices entries for the 23rd and 25th October of a particular year and therefore assumes that during the year in question the month of October did not contain a 24th day. When he explains this to a friend he cannot understand the humorous reaction he receives.

Keyword
Observation

Element
Air

Planet
Venus ♀

DEGREE 18

Keyword
Appearances

Element
Air

Planet
Venus ♀

Too high and exposed for plants to be able to withstand the severity of the climate, a mountain peak appears stark and barren. A closer inspection of the rocky outcrop reveals nooks and crannies where nesting birds find protection and shelter. The lack of foliage close by is no detriment to the birds, who can fly elsewhere to feed.

DEGREE 19

The doorway of a building is neither outside nor inside but can be considered to be both. When the door is shut and you are outside, you cannot perceive what is within. Conversely, if you are inside the building with the door shut, you cannot experience what is without. Only when you stand between the two can you be aware of both realities.

Keyword
Dualities

Element
Air

Planet
Venus ♀

DEGREE 20

Keyword
Relatedness

Element
Air

Planet
Venus ♀

A worker approaches his employer to ask for a raise. The employer explains in detail the financial constraints governing the lack of money available. The employee mulls over the problem on the way home on the bus, which is passed at the first set of traffic lights by the employer in his large, expensive luxury saloon car.

DEGREE 21

Arriving at the house of a rich merchant, a messenger is tired after the long journey. The master of the house insists that the messenger rest and eat before delivering his news. During the intervening period the merchant, who is elderly, is suddenly taken ill and dies. The messenger cannot now deliver the words he was charged with, so the news, good or bad, is irrelevant.

Keyword
Consideration

Element
Air

Planet
Uranus ♅

Keyword
Selective

Element
Air

Planet
Uranus ♅

DEGREE 22

At a holiday centre, a ventriloquist's skill has a tremendous effect on a child who visits the centre during the summer. Years later the child, now a young adult, once again meets the ventriloquist. Memories of the artiste have faded, but he immediately recognises the puppets when he is shown them.

DEGREE 23

To save space in his farmyard and fields a farmer builds his hay ricks larger than has been the practice for generations, and in close proximity to each other. When one of the ricks bursts into flames, all the others catch fire and all the hay is destroyed in minutes.

Keyword
Conformity

Element
Air

Planet
Uranus ♅

Keyword
Diversity

Element
Air

Planet
Uranus ♅

DEGREE 24

Travelling the country and rarely stopping for more than a week in one place, an able and hard-working craftsman is regularly offered permanent employment but always refuses. He does so because his work and friendship, he believes, will never be a source of irritation to others if all see him as new, interesting and a source of curiosity.

DEGREE 25

In the heavy, smoke-laden atmosphere of a plush hotel restaurant, members of an exclusive club sit captivated by the verbal dexterity, wit and impeccable diction of a great orator. Meeting the speaker later, club members are surprised to be confronted by a shy, retiring individual with a pronounced stammer.

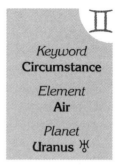

Keyword
Circumstance

Element
Air

Planet
Uranus ♅

DEGREE 26

Keyword
Perspective

Element
Air

Planet
Uranus ♅

With a deft flick of the wrist, the conjuror produces a live dove from beneath a silk square. All the members of the audience are well aware of the deception they are witness to, but nevertheless they watch eagerly. One onlooker is disappointed, however, because he knows how the trick is performed.

DEGREE 27

Born within minutes of each other, a pair of identical twins are separated shortly after birth. One rises high in life, whilst the other occupies a more lowly position. Despite their differing fortunes, their appearance and basic characteristics remain absolutely identical until the day of their death.

Keyword
Inevitability

Element
Air

Planet
Uranus ♅

DEGREE 28

Keyword
Suspicion

Element
Air

Planet
Uranus ♅

During a war, a town is besieged but has plenty of supplies and could hold out for a considerable period. A rumour starts that infiltrators have been planted in the community. The suspicion of hostility thus created weakens the collective strength of the town so much that the inhabitants become less disciplined and the attackers are able to gain entry.

DEGREE 29

Greyhounds on a racing track do not necessarily appreciate that they are competing. For them the objective is to catch the automatic hare that always stays in front of them. Time after time they fail to catch the hare and yet on each occasion they still endeavour to do so.

Keyword
Tenacity

Element
Air

Planet
Uranus ♅

DEGREE 30

Keyword
Observation

Element
Air

Planet
Uranus ♅

Because of differing atmospheric pressures, the needle of a barometer can point in various directions. This indicates the most likely weather. In the eyes of those who look at the device it would appear that the mechanism has some skill to actually predict the future. The painted face of the barometer hides the mechanism behind.

CANCER

♋

Can the Sun stand even for a moment in heaven when movement is irrepressible? So it appears. Look again and search diligently with the no-mind that encompasses complete knowing. All that is perceived is the farthest extent of the pendulum's swing, beyond which all physical laws cease to have accustomed validity. Here is the everlasting now.

Moon	Sun	Mercury	Venus	Mars
☽	☉	☿	♀	♂
Jupiter	Saturn	Uranus	Neptune	Pluto
♃	♄	♅	♆	♇

DEGREE 1

The amount of information that a baby absorbs immediately after birth is colossal. To look at such an apparently helpless, innocent and feeble creature, few people would guess the incredible sifting, sorting and correlation of knowledge and information that is taking place.

Keyword
Hidden

Element
Water

Planet
Moon ☽

DEGREE 2

Keyword
Experience

Element
Water

Planet
Moon ☽

Because of the length of time he has been in the trade and the skill he has amassed, the baker does not need to weigh the ingredients he mixes for batches of bread each day. His new assistant, after a short while, tries to copy his employer's example, with disastrous results. The bread is too salty and does not rise sufficiently.

DEGREE 3

After some months employed in a busy public house, a pretty and friendly barmaid has learned not to take too seriously the teasing she receives from some of the regulars. The strange fact is that when she meets the same individuals in the street, they are often shy in her company.

Keyword
Alternatives

Element
Water

Planet
Moon ☽

DEGREE 4

Keyword
Hesitance

Element
Water

Planet
Moon ☽

Tossed by stormy seas in mid-Atlantic many weeks from home, a round-the-world yachtswoman considers her reasons for undertaking such an arduous solo task. She is wet, miserable and cold, and cannot at present quite understand her own motivation. It was clear enough when she embarked and will be so again once the journey is over.

DEGREE 5

A small brook that meanders and slowly follows a centuries-chosen path, is destined eventually to become the raging torrent that surges on impatiently to the sea. The brook is the torrent and also the sea. For though the name and the force differ, the water involved is the same.

Keyword
Transformation

Element
Water

Planet
Moon ☽

DEGREE 6

Keyword
Vulnerable

Element
Water

Planet
Moon ☽

Safe inside its protective adopted shell, the hermit crab's only basic vulnerability lies in its inability to remain the same size. Periodically it has to find a larger shell and must, for a short time at least, leave itself open to attack, bereft of its protective armour.

DEGREE 7

Left to burn in a still and quiet room, the flame of a candle does not waver or fluctuate. Should the smallest of draughts be allowed to pervade the calm air of the room, the candle flame bends against the current of air, consuming the wax unevenly and spilling it unburned.

Keyword
Fluctuation

Element
Water

Planet
Moon ☽

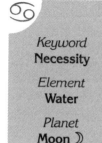

DEGREE 8

Keyword
Necessity

Element
Water

Planet
Moon ☽

Having performed its mating ritual, a drake no longer takes any interest in the rearing of its family. The duck herself patiently builds a nest, lays the eggs and sits on them, not to mention taking care of the chicks once they have hatched. Yet for all his selfish behaviour, the process still could not take place without the drake's contribution.

DEGREE 9

For many centuries it was a total mystery where eels disappeared to when they undertook their long journey down to the sea. Like many migratory aquatic species, although they travel huge distances – possibly as far as the Sargasso Sea – eels can still find their way back to the very stream where they themselves were spawned.

Keyword
Instinct

Element
Water

Planet
Moon ☽

DEGREE 10

Keyword
Cohesion

Element
Water

Planet
Moon ☽

Gathered together only once each year, a certain family can feel secure, even if only temporarily, in their collective identity. Individual members of the family rarely have any contact at all throughout most of the year, but on this one evening their individual lives are of little significance.

DEGREE 11

After long hours of patient waiting on the river bank, a fisherman decides to take some lunch. Moving no more than a few feet away from the rod, he sees the float dip for the first time all day. Before he can get back to the rod his bait has been taken and the fish has escaped.

Keyword
Attentiveness

Element
Water

Planet
Mars ♂

DEGREE 12

Keyword
Realisation

Element
Water

Planet
Mars ♂

A home-worker is bored with the day-to-day routines that are her lot and decides to take a part-time job in a local factory. Very soon the sheer monotony of her task at the factory, which simply necessitates pressing a button, helps her to appreciate the variety that her housework could sometimes present.

DEGREE 13

The elderly caretaker takes his usual evening stroll around the deserted building. Although the property has been condemned and is due to be demolished in a matter of days, he still replaces spent light bulbs and carefully sweeps the corridors. It is his intention that the building should be spotless when the demolition team arrives to destroy his world for good.

Keyword
Diligence

Element
Water

Planet
Mars ♂

DEGREE 14

Keyword
Trust

Element
Water

Planet
Mars ♂

For many years the beam streaming forth from a lighthouse protecting a rocky outcrop has prevented countless ships from coming to grief. One night the mechanism becomes faulty, and it takes several hours for it to be repaired. The night in question has a full moon and consequently no ships run onto the rocks for they can see the silhouette of the lighthouse.

DEGREE 15

Since mankind first lifted its head to gaze at the evening sky, the Moon has been the object of the closest scrutiny and reverence. Despite the fact that the Moon shines in reflected glory, courtesy of the Sun, its significance to the Earth and to man has always been individual and unique.

Keyword
Self-sufficiency

Element
Water

Planet
Mars ♂

DEGREE 16

Keyword
Precaution

Element
Water

Planet
Mars ♂

On many occasions, despite her skill and training, a midwife does very little when presiding at the birth of a baby that any other reasonably competent individual could not achieve. Her presence offers confidence against the contingency that problems may just possibly arise.

DEGREE 17

A new recruit into the merchant navy is warned by all his shipmates of the rigours of sea sickness, which they assure him strikes all new mariners. The recruit is surprised that he does not experience such problems, despite a rolling and pitching ocean on the first night at sea. Later he has need to see the First Officer but is turned away because the man is suffering from sea sickness.

Keyword
Paradox

Element
Water

Planet
Mars ♂

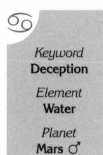

Keyword
Deception

Element
Water

Planet
Mars ♂

DEGREE 18

Facing a difficult political problem, a queen whose husband is too ill to make decisions, decides to preside in his absence. Those in attendance believe the instructions that they are given to be from the King himself. Thanks to the deception, enemies of the state never discover the potential vulnerability caused by the King's illness.

DEGREE 19

Washing day sees members of a community boiling gallons of water. It takes many hours to do this, and it would be laborious work save for the companionship and co-operative efforts of the people involved. Their congenial banter and willingness to support each other makes an unpleasant task into a socially meaningful event.

Keyword
Reliance

Element
Water

Planet
Mars ♂

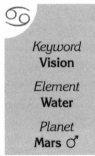

Keyword
Vision

Element
Water

Planet
Mars ♂

DEGREE 20

Alone for most of the night with no company, a solitary night-watchman spends hours staring into the glow of his brazier, reliving events in his past. The pictures in the coals are a comfort to him and make a lonely night pass quickly.

DEGREE 21

A delivery boy is stopped by the police when on his early evening rounds and accused of having no rear light on his bicycle. A closer inspection reveals that the bulb is shining as brightly as ever but that the reflective backing is rusty and dull.

Keyword
Discovery

Element
Water

Planet
Neptune ♆

DEGREE 22

Keyword
Options

Element
Water

Planet
Neptune ♆

Like clear glass in any ordinary house, the richly ornamented stained glass of churches serves the primary function of letting light into the building. Though in this sense both windows are the same, no one would suggest that the stained glass can be defined by this function.

DEGREE 23

Having arrived at the same port many times, the Captain of a cargo ship has never totally understood the necessity of having a harbour pilot aboard to steer what seems to be a quite straightforward course. One dark and turbulent night he is grateful for the pilot's expert knowledge and realises that circumstances can throw up many variables.

Keyword
Confirmation

Element
Water

Planet
Neptune ♆

DEGREE 24

Keyword
Perspective

Element
Water

Planet
Neptune ♆

Looking at a tree from a distance a casual observer has no comprehension of the many processes taking place behind the bark. He cannot observe the sap rising or falling, neither can he view the growing processes which take place continually.

DEGREE 25

On a busy seafront a shrimp seller does brisk business with holiday-makers who are anxious to try the freshly caught produce of the local ocean. The shrimp seller does not inform the public with whom she deals that the merchandise was caught days ago and on the other side of the world.

Keyword
Assumption

Element
Water

Planet
Neptune ♆

DEGREE 26

Keyword
Recognition

Element
Water

Planet
Neptune ♆

Graceful and majestic, a willow bends in apparent supplication, bowing its regal branches towards the life-giving water that has allowed it to gain strength, whilst at the same time preserving its supple nature.

DEGREE 27

A sheep dog at work displays a kind of controlled natural behaviour. It appears to follow the shepherd's instructions to the letter in rounding up and returning sheep to him. In the wild it would use the same procedure to head prey towards the rest of the pack whilst hunting.

Keyword
Utilisation

Element
Water

Planet
Neptune ♆

DEGREE 28

Keyword
Conformity

Element
Water

Planet
Neptune ♆

Because a mother fails to be consistent in the way she treats her child, he is confused and fails to respond to any discipline, never really knowing what is expected of him. When in the company of more consistent adults, the child is comfortable and well behaved.

DEGREE 29

In the depths of a thick tangled jungle an explorer happens upon a hitherto unknown tribe of great composure and natural beauty. After spending some enjoyable days in their company, he deliberately loses the map reference to their whereabouts.

Keyword
Preservation

Element
Water

Planet
Neptune ♆

DEGREE 30

Keyword
Belief

Element
Water

Planet
Neptune ♆

A very rich and slightly eccentric person rents a market stall in the local town and spends the day not selling a commodity but trying to give away new bank notes to the shoppers. When he takes stock at the end of the day he is disappointed to see that only two or three people have suspended their preconceptions about life enough to accept his genuine and generous offer.

LEO

♌

*A power is thrown down and the
vanquisher becomes the vanquished.
Humility drinks freely at the well of
heroism, unaware and unconcerned
about an account of the battle that few
know to be falsehood. The water is
pure, sweet and satisfying.*

Moon	Sun	Mercury	Venus	Mars
☽	☉	☿	♀	♂
Jupiter	Saturn	Uranus	Neptune	Pluto
♃	♄	♅	♆	♇

DEGREE 1

The animator is aware that his individual pictures, when filmed in order and replayed, will appear to be moving in an ordered sequence. Through the medium, events impossible for actors to perform can be created; an illusion can become a reality.

Keyword
Illusion

Element
Fire

Planet
Sun ☉

DEGREE 2

Keyword
Concentration

Element
Fire

Planet
Sun ☉

Boasting of his success on the track, the racing driver now on the road in a private car is so busy talking that he fails to negotiate a bend in the road and runs the vehicle into a ditch.

DEGREE 3

Waiting in the yard of his busy factory, the owner looks at his pocket watch and admonishes those workers who do not arrive on time. At the end of the day he does not thank those workers who work a few extra minutes, concerned to finish properly the tasks in which they are involved.

Keyword
Fairness

Element
Fire

Planet
Sun ☉

DEGREE 4

Keyword
Transcendent

Element
Fire

Planet
Sun ☉

Throughout history the circle has been used to portray perpetual existence. It is the very essence of unchanging certainty and the promise of universal eternity. In mathematics, however, the circle is worth absolutely – nothing.

DEGREE 5

Gifted, or alternatively cursed, with an over-sensitive conscience, a child who has argued with her parents tries to make amends by willingly running errands and endeavouring to be generally useful. The forgiveness in the parents is their willingness to allow the child to behave in this way.

Keyword
Acceptance

Element
Fire

Planet
Sun ☉

DEGREE 6

Keyword
Perspective

Element
Fire

Planet
Sun ☉

An individual walking along a narrow beam placed upon the ground experiences no fear of falling from the beam and so accomplishes the task easily. If the length of wood were placed high in the air, only extensive training could blot out the consequences of a mistake.

DEGREE 7

Two workers are overseen by the same foreman. Because they have different personalities, he encourages one but often reprimands the other. Each worker knows a different foreman, yet they both view the same man.

Keyword
Reality

Element
Fire

Planet
Sun ☉

DEGREE 8

Keyword
Probability

Element
Fire

Planet
Sun ☉

Because he has the power of life and death over his subjects, a king is viewed by them as being all powerful. The monarch himself is possessed of a scolding wife, and the wife's greatest fear is the power inherent in the people if they should choose to unite and rise.

DEGREE 9

Many people accuse a rich philanthropist of being false because they believe that the good he does for the poor is merely a means of feeding his own ego and justifying his riches, yet without his generosity many people might have starved.

Keyword
Motive

Element
Fire

Planet
Sun ☉

DEGREE 10

Keyword
Opportunity

Element
Fire

Planet
Sun ☉

Having lost all senior officers in a battle, a hitherto quiet and ineffectual junior officer assumes command of a group of soldiers. Immediately the officer proves to be a competent leader at a time of great difficulty.

DEGREE 11

A lavish state banquet is held to entertain foreign emissaries who have arrived to try to negotiate a peace treaty between two antagonistic factions. Although the country holding the feast is poor and can ill afford the expense, the treaty is negotiated and the ensuing peace allows economic growth to improve the country's financial standing.

Keyword
Eventuality

Element
Fire

Planet
Jupiter ♃

DEGREE 12

Keyword
Confidence

Element
Fire

Planet
Jupiter ♃

Despite warnings from all sides about the certainty of a difficult economic situation ahead, a businessman optimistically keeps ploughing money into his factory. When the minor slump is over he is able to expand the business quickly because he did not run down his capacity or work force.

DEGREE 13

Although it presents a magnificent spectacle, the display of a peacock is of little use or significance unless there are females in the vicinity. The entire procedure is an elaborate mating ritual.

Keyword
Flamboyance

Element
Fire

Planet
Jupiter ♃

DEGREE 14

Keyword
Lethargy

Element
Fire

Planet
Jupiter ♃

Despite its power and co-operative hunting ability, the lion is essentially a lazy animal. When not hungry, it spends most of its time lying in the sun or idling away the hours in play. It will even steal the catch of some other predator, given the opportunity.

DEGREE 15

Universally speaking, our Sun is not particularly large, yet without it neither the Earth nor any living creature upon it could exist. We are totally dependent on this star and yet only a minute fraction of the Sun's power reaches the Earth. Most is lost to the endless depths of icy space.

Keyword
Dependence

Element
Fire

Planet
Jupiter ♃

DEGREE 16

Keyword
Realisation

Element
Fire

Planet
Jupiter ♃

An ageing theatre is condemned to be demolished. The situation is the cause of angry protests by local residents who remember the theatre's former glory. The building has been closed for many years but only when the intention to knock it down becomes clear do the protests start.

DEGREE 17

Bystanders watch with interest the filming of a scene destined for a popular television series. The fact that the watchers see stage directions and hear the participants talking and behaving as their true life selves does not undermine their belief in the characters as they will ultimately appear in the finished programme.

Keyword
Imagination

Element
Fire

Planet
Jupiter ♃

DEGREE 18

Keyword
Delusion

Element
Fire

Planet
Jupiter ♃

On the platform at a political meeting, a politician reads his speech. In dramatic tones he deplores the conduct of the present government of his country, extolling the virtue of the party he is certain will soon be brought to power. He has read the same speech so many times before that he has actually begun to believe that one day things will genuinely be different.

DEGREE 19

A young woman arrives in her home port after a protracted period abroad, where she has been successful financially. She is pleased with her efforts and has been yearning for her homeland for a long time. In a very short while she realises that in her absence either she or her country has changed, and so she sets off on her journeys again.

Keyword
Expectation

Element
Fire

Planet
Jupiter ♃

DEGREE 20

Keyword
Revision

Element
Fire

Planet
Jupiter ♃

Having spent all his life teaching a particular branch of philosophy to his students, a well-known teacher suddenly changes his entire point of view. He is aware that he cannot 'unteach' his former students but is equally certain that his revised viewpoint is correct.

DEGREE 21

For many months a bounty hunter has tracked a wanted criminal and has at last cornered him in a small town. The transgressor has built himself a peaceful and law-abiding life, having repented his past follies. The bounty hunter sees only the money involved and insists on returning the criminal for trial.

Keyword
Karma

Element
Fire

Planet
Mars ♂

DEGREE 22

Keyword
Tunnel vision

Element
Fire

Planet
Mars ♂

Having joined a religious sect that fundamentally disagrees with her early learning, a teenager finds she has become the cause of bitterness within her family. Though they agree that her moral code and basic beliefs are sound, they cannot accept her personal need to follow a different path.

DEGREE 23

There are many metals more valuable than gold in terms of their potential uses, and yet throughout countless ages men have been willing to steal, cheat and even kill on its account. Like any other metal it is only precious in relation to man's need to possess it.

Keyword
Avarice

Element
Fire

Planet
Mars ♂

DEGREE 24

Keyword
Misunderstanding

Element
Fire

Planet
Mars ♂

Attempting to show his genuine affection in the only way open to him, a millionaire spends vast amounts on securing the love of his daughter. He is heartbroken when she runs off with a penniless nobody. He cannot understand the difference between the love he showed his daughter and the love she ran away to find.

DEGREE 25

A visitor to a foreign country finds himself in trouble with the law over certain remarks he has made regarding the government. His intention was not to cause trouble, he was merely joking. He failed to recognise that the culture was very different from his own and that under certain circumstances a joke can appear to be an insult.

Keyword
Forethought

Element
Fire

Planet
Mars ♂

DEGREE 26

Keyword
Need

Element
Fire

Planet
Mars ♂

Having for many years charged nothing for his services, a healer is at last forced by economic necessity to demand a fee. Though he is certain that people may think twice about consulting him, he is surprised to discover that his clientele doubles in a matter of days.

DEGREE 27

Utilising a toy gun, a robber holds up a bank and demands that a bag be filled with money. The teller turns away to fill the bag. Later, when the thief has a chance to check his haul, he discovers that he has been given nothing but useless pieces of blank paper.

Keyword
Justice

Element
Fire

Planet
Mars ♂

DEGREE 28

Keyword
Specialisation

Element
Fire

Planet
Mars ♂

A general who has been successful in many campaigns and is much decorated by his nation, takes part in a military coup to overthrow what he considers to be a repressive government. Unfortunately, he is a better soldier than he is a politician and within weeks is himself displaced and totally discredited.

DEGREE 29

Whilst performing all season for only the pleasure of the competition, a gifted young athlete does extremely well. Representing her country at the Olympics, however, her nerve fails. In a subsequent event she forgets the circumstances of the competition and starts to enjoy herself. In the process she wins a medal.

Keyword
Proportions

Element
Fire

Planet
Mars ♂

DEGREE 30

♌

Keyword
Necessity

Element
Fire

Planet
Mars ♂

Domestic cats, even if well fed, rarely lose the ability or desire to hunt. Birds or rodents often fall prey to this efficient and merciless predator. The advantage of retaining the hunting skill could mean the difference between life and death if at any time a particular cat were forced to fend for itself.

VIRGO

♍

The world turns from season to season;
what was once sterile is now bearing
fruit. Out of nothing comes forth all the
bounty that nature can bestow. Apart
and separate, the word and the principle
grow in unison, following a determined
path and never being diverted by the
mind of man. The pattern may not be
swayed but it can be understood.
Through understanding comes
knowledge; from knowledge springs
the solution.

Moon ☽	Sun ☉	Mercury ☿	Venus ♀	Mars ♂
Jupiter ♃	Saturn ♄	Uranus ♅	Neptune ♆	Pluto ♇

DEGREE 1

♍

Working long into the night, an accountant checks and re-checks row after row of figures. He is certain that they contain an error which, despite his avid scrutiny, he cannot find. Eventually he concedes temporary defeat and goes home. Next day, fresh and alert, he discovers the mistake in minutes.

Keyword
Fatigue

Element
Earth

Planet
Mercury ☿

♍

DEGREE 2

Keyword
Persistence

Element
Earth

Planet
Mercury ☿

A great breakthrough is announced concerning treatment of a terrible disease, the effects of which have incapacitated tens of thousands of people. To the eyes of the public the discovery of the new drug seems like instant success, though to the people concerned it represents years of painstaking research.

DEGREE 3

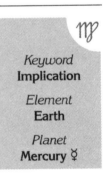

♍

Viewed on paper, the architect's plan for a new high-rise development appears to be a superb answer to housing shortages. His plans fail to show the social isolation, filth, graffiti and vandalism that will mar the objectives of his concept.

Keyword
Implication

Element
Earth

Planet
Mercury ☿

♍

DEGREE 4

Keyword
Alternative

Element
Earth

Planet
Mercury ☿

Alone in his office, the astrologer carefully checks his calculations and realises that his client is due for a fairly difficult period to come and that he must now decide how specific to be in his consultation. Ten minutes prior to the consultation he finally tears up the offending chart. His conscience pricks, but fortunately the client fails to meet the appointment

DEGREE 5

After months of effort a hard-working author puts the finishing touches to a long and complex novel. Since the book is more or less assured of general success, the writer could take a long break before commencing a subsequent work, but through the last couple of chapters of his present book new ideas have started to emerge which force him to begin immediately.

♍

Keyword
Immediacy

Element
Earth

Planet
Mercury ☿

♍

Keyword
Truth

Element
Earth

Planet
Mercury ☿

DEGREE 6

In a temple situated in the Western world stands a Buddha that was a present from an old and revered establishment in the Far East. The statue shows a happy rotund figure, serene and all wise. Although the cultural differences between East and West are obvious, the Buddha still smiles in the busy industrial city.

DEGREE 7

Intent on the book she is reading, a child is walking to the shops, on an errand for her parents. She is absorbed by the tale and, not concentrating, is knocked down by a car. Although only shaken, the child has learned a valuable lesson about apparent realities.

♍

Keyword
Concentration

Element
Earth

Planet
Mercury ☿

♍

Keyword
Quest

Element
Earth

Planet
Mercury ☿

DEGREE 8

Deep in the virtually impenetrable jungle, an ordered and well planned garden grows behind a high wall. In the midst of the garden is a maze of great complexity. The jungle makes the garden almost impossible to find and the maze is difficult to traverse. In the centre of the maze is a locked box. The box is empty.

DEGREE 9

♍

Within the Victorian household, a governess was a social outcast. She was not one of the family, nor was she one of the servants, and she was usually forced to spend most of her time in the company of children. On her day off each week she could at least travel to a local town, there to enjoy the same anonymity as everyone else.

Keyword
Position

Element
Earth

Planet
Mercury ☿

♍

DEGREE 10

Keyword
Attention

Element
Earth

Planet
Mercury ☿

Because of the cultural as well as the language problems, a young interpreter is having a difficult time assisting two high-powered emissaries at an international conference. She is aware that she could cause offence by a misinterpretation but at the same time must ensure that she does not over-embellish or otherwise alter the fundamental meaning of phrases from either side.

DEGREE 11

♍

During his rounds a postman is depressed by the number of bills and circulars that he is obliged to deliver, and senses that as a result his arrival is not always welcome. Without thinking, he passes a house where he hardly ever calls, the lonely occupant of which would be pleased with a communication of any kind.

Keyword
Communicate

Element
Earth

Planet
Saturn ♄

♍

DEGREE 12

Keyword
Values

Element
Earth

Planet
Saturn ♄

A merchant on business in a distant and strange land is allowed to take a look in the treasure store of a rich and ancient temple. As he scans the wealth of gold and silver, he makes a mental assessment of the value of some of the items. Such a valuation would never be possible in the eyes of the monk who shows him round, for he sees only spiritual worth in the collection.

DEGREE 13

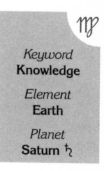

Divided from his neighbours by a high fence, a householder feels secure within his own house and garden. One day a high wind demolishes the fence and for the first time the householder talks in depth with his neighbour. So much does he enjoy the conversation that the next fence he builds is considerably smaller.

Keyword
Knowledge

Element
Earth

Planet
Saturn ♄

DEGREE 14

♍

Keyword
Procrastination

Element
Earth

Planet
Saturn ♄

Owing to pressure of work, a printer delays printing a medical book that has just been released. His present labour is nothing more important than a frivolous and unsavoury magazine, and while he works on it, people who could gain real benefit from the new treatments in the medical volume continue to suffer.

DEGREE 15

Having read thousands of manuscripts in her career, a literary agent one day passes up a book which, if she did but know it, is destined to become a colossal best seller. This is the first manuscript ever sent to her that she has failed to scrutinise properly. She ensures that such a mistake is never repeated.

Keyword
Distraction

Element
Earth

Planet
Saturn ♄

DEGREE 16

♍

Keyword
Blindness

Element
Earth

Planet
Saturn ♄

A certain business executive is given to underestimating the value of his secretary. Despite the tremendous assistance she gives him, he is often offhand and rude to her. When he is on holiday, business continues as usual, but when she is away the work piles up awaiting her return.

DEGREE 17

During a crucial tennis match and with the game all but even, one of the players becomes extremely temperamental and vehemently questions the call of 'out' from a line judge. Even though in his heart he knows the call was good, the tennis player goes on arguing until he totally upsets his own equilibrium and subsequently loses the game.

♍

Keyword
Self-defeat

Element
Earth

Planet
Saturn ♄

♍

Keyword
Perception

Element
Earth

Planet
Saturn ♄

DEGREE 18

For years a philosopher spends his time trying to assess the essential truths and correct the failings of humanity. Never having worked outside the educational environment and rarely mixing socially with people below his own intellect, he fails dismally to understand why all his efforts are doomed to failure.

DEGREE 19

Having always been subject to a rigid moral code, a young woman has chosen to remain a virgin until the day before her marriage. Her new husband, who has not been so abstemious, nevertheless respects her point of view. He is surprised when on the night before the wedding she breaks her self-imposed vow with only a few hours left before the ceremony.

♍

Keyword
Choice

Element
Earth

Planet
Saturn ♄

♍

Keyword
Vision

Element
Earth

Planet
Saturn ♄

DEGREE 20

With an over-large case load and little or no assistance, a social worker toils many hours beyond her expected working week and, despite her tiredness, genuinely tries to help her clients. To each of the people she assists there are no other clients and they see the social worker as belonging solely to them.

DEGREE 21

The parachutist's sense of reality changes very little when, having just left the aircraft, he hangs high above the ground. It is only when he drops down and his surroundings telescope that the landing site, which when viewed from the aircraft was only a small part of a whole, becomes the most important consideration.

Keyword
Alteration

Element
Earth

Planet
Venus ♀

DEGREE 22

Keyword
Integration

Element
Earth

Planet
Venus ♀

Bees have a sophisticated and efficient means of communication. Constant touching of antennae, one insect to another, can pass sensory messages extremely quickly. The hive could not exist without information regarding the location of food supplies.

DEGREE 23

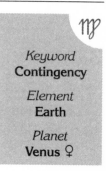

Being one of the strongest of the English Tudor monarchs, Queen Elizabeth I was considered by most of her subjects and by the Church to be on favourable terms with the Almighty. When important decisions had to be made, this fact did not prevent her from consulting an astrologer, who together with all such luminaries was frowned upon by the church.

Keyword
Contingency

Element
Earth

Planet
Venus ♀

DEGREE 24

Keyword
Hidden

Element
Earth

Planet
Venus ♀

Inside and outside Europe, Paris is regarded with a reverence granted specifically to this one city. Its treasures, sights and history give it a reputation for being one of the artistic and cultural gems of the world. Despite this fact, it has brothels, run-down housing and social problems in abundance.

DEGREE 25

♍

During the middle ages the wild boar was considered one of the most prized animals, both for its flesh and the sport it offered. Capturing the creature was no easy task. Armed with vicious tusks and possessing a mean and fiery disposition, a boar is well able to kill a man with one charge.

Keyword
Defence

Element
Earth

Planet
Venus ♀

♍

DEGREE 26

Keyword
Observe

Element
Earth

Planet
Venus ♀

Down a quiet country road a cyclist slowly pedals, drinking in the picturesque surroundings. He covers little distance compared to a motorist, who is able to arrive at his destination much faster. The motorist, however, has to concentrate so hard that he has little time to appreciate nature's beauty, nor can he smell or hear the subtle signposts that mark his route as the cyclist does.

DEGREE 27

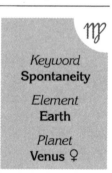

A person can talk incessantly for the sake of the sound he or she makes, but this is no sign that the speaker says anything that is worth knowing. On the other hand, a casual remark can carry tremendous significance on occasions.

Keyword
Spontaneity

Element
Earth

Planet
Venus ♀

♍

DEGREE 28

Keyword
Coincidence

Element
Earth

Planet
Venus ♀

The silence of the library is shattered by a young librarian who accidentally drops a large pile of books. Embarrassed, she stoops to pick them up, noticing with a wry smile that the last book is entitled *How to Make an Instant Impression on Others.*

DEGREE 29

Lying for days in a coma, a girl injured in a motor accident eventually regains consciousness. She cannot remember the accident or the ensuing period, although she is assured by the nursing staff that the accident has occurred and the period has elapsed. She accepts on logical grounds the facts as told to her, but they can never be substantiated by her personal awareness.

Keyword
Time

Element
Earth

Planet
Venus ♀

DEGREE 30

♍

Keyword
Precision

Element
Earth

Planet
Venus ♀

A young man is discovered one day by a friend, working on the tiny pilot from one of his model aircraft. The modeller, who is holding a magnifying glass and a super-fine paintbrush, is asked what he is labouring at so intently. It turns out that he is painting medal ribbons on the pilot's jacket, though the figure will be barely discernible when fitted into the cockpit.

LIBRA

♎

The heart and the feather upon the
balance are etched in stone, frozen in
time and safe in the darkness for
millennia. Locked into the sediment
since the world began, what is their
reality now beyond the mind? The same
feather could balance the whole earth
until the end of time.

Moon	Sun	Mercury	Venus	Mars
☽	☉	☿	♀	♂
Jupiter	Saturn	Uranus	Neptune	Pluto
♃	♄	♅	♆	♇

DEGREE 1

A spring balance needs no counter-weight. The object being weighed is balanced by a spring housed within the machine itself. The accuracy of the device depends entirely upon the design and manufacture of its components. If it registers the wrong weight on the scale, the machine is of no use whatsoever.

Keyword
Inventive

Element
Air

Planet
Venus ♀

DEGREE 2

Keyword
Fineness

Element
Air

Planet
Venus ♀

Trying to capture the essential three-dimensional characteristics of an athlete, a sculptor tries again and again to perfect the clay model. Eventually the artist slightly changes the stance of her model and discovers that the new pose is less difficult to translate into the medium.

DEGREE 3

Feeling genuine compassion for urchins who sleep rough in the street, a Victorian philanthropist sets up an orphanage for such children. Though now fed and clothed, in their patron's absence the children are subject to a harsh form of discipline and humiliation that they never encountered whilst living rough.

Keyword
Alternative

Element
Air

Planet
Venus ♀

DEGREE 4

Keyword
Comprehend

Element
Air

Planet
Venus ♀

Prior to a concert, a pianist composes himself and practises finger exercises in his dressing room. Every performance is as unnerving as the first and each one takes a great toll on his nervous system. Only when the concert is over does the maestro realise, in some small measure, what his gifts are.

DEGREE 5

Long after the reality of a romantic and happy evening has passed, a young woman, who on that first night encountered the joy of love, remembers the warmth of a caress and the heady perfume of the evening air. The romance may not last, but the memories will.

Keyword
Recall

Element
Air

Planet
Venus ♀

Keyword
Interlude

Element
Air

Planet
Venus ♀

DEGREE 6

The rut is over and soon the proud stags will lose their antlers. What were, during that brief period, wild, aggressive and dangerous animals, now revert to being merely a component part of the herd. They can be observed grazing pensively with the rest of their kind.

DEGREE 7

Man has often sensed the intelligence inherent in his aquatic cousin, the dolphin, but the language to communicate with these bright creatures may never be discovered. Perhaps this is because, despite our similarities in some ways, we simply have nothing to say to each other.

Keyword
Separate

Element
Air

Planet
Venus ♀

Keyword
Flexible

Element
Air

Planet
Venus ♀

DEGREE 8

Well aware that on this evening his act is not being well received, a comedian continues with his usual routine, despite the fact that the audience is restive and even insulting. On the previous night, however, the same jokes had brought the house down.

DEGREE 9

Because of his artistic interests and general appearance, a particular young man is often thought of as being effeminate. Though most people recognise his right to be whatever he wishes, one or two ridicule and taunt him. Eventually, tired of the harassment, the man moves away from the district, but he finds that wherever he travels the ignorant few continue to be intolerant.

Keyword
Escape

Element
Air

Planet
Venus ♀

DEGREE 10

Keyword
Refuge

Element
Air

Planet
Venus ♀

Customers marvel at the colourful display of blooms in the florist's window, which brighten up a cold and cheerless winter's day. Many of the flowers are artificial, but even these can be appreciated against the snow and sleet of January.

DEGREE 11

A woman unpopular with many of her associates is accused of being flirtatious to the point of trying to steal her friends' partners. Because it is her basic nature to behave the way she does, she finds it hard to change, or even to understand why on the one hand she gets on so well with men but on the other cannot seem to make friends within her own gender.

Keyword
Search

Element
Air

Planet
Uranus ♅

DEGREE 12

Keyword
Understanding

Element
Air

Planet
Uranus ♅

Spending much time at court, a young duke has the reputation of being both gallant and charming. He is elected as the queen's champion and henceforth defends her honour in all his actions. His own wife leads a miserable life in the country, with few diversions and little or nothing to occupy her mind.

DEGREE 13

In the confines of a small hotel during the out of season period, it is obvious that a young couple who have recently arrived are on their honeymoon. It is the couple themselves who telegraph the fact, so obviously do they endeavour to hide it. Were they to act as if they had just married, perhaps nobody would notice.

Keyword
Disguise

Element
Air

Planet
Uranus ♅

DEGREE 14

Keyword
Utilise

Element
Air

Planet
Uranus ♅

If you were left an ornament to take care of by a friend whilst he or she were away for a protracted period, would you hide the object in a cupboard, fearing for its safety if burglars called, or would you put it on display to enhance your home and remind you of the friend who will eventually return?

DEGREE 15

Three astronauts look down from their orbiting spacecraft to the Earth far below. Their previous lives have all been very different from each other, and although as a result of this experience they will all change greatly, it will be in radically different ways. Nevertheless they all look towards the Earth with the same love.

Keyword
Communion

Element
Air

Planet
Uranus ♅

DEGREE 16

Keyword
Microcosm

Element
Air

Planet
Uranus ♅

Despite the noise and clatter of an unruly class, a young and inexperienced school teacher does her best to get on with the lesson in hand. She knows that one child near the back of the class is showing interest, and in the mind of the teacher the rest of the class ceases to exist. For the child, too, the surrounding commotion is blotted out by her interest and desire to learn.

DEGREE 17

It has always been considered a necessary prerequisite of a certain carnival that the maiden, taking part as the queen of the ceremony, should be pure in every sense of the word. Because of the delicacy of the situation, after a while the question is no longer asked directly. In order to ensure the maiden's purity, a younger girl is chosen with each passing year.

Keyword
Truth

Element
Air

Planet
Uranus ♅

DEGREE 18

Keyword
Perspective

Element
Air

Planet
Uranus ♅

Resting backstage after his performance, an opera singer condescends to see two fans who have been waiting patiently outside for some time. The event is of little consequence to the international star, for he sees admirers almost every day, but it is a once-in-a-lifetime occasion for the fans.

DEGREE 19

A party is in full swing when a neighbour arrives to try to quieten the event down, for he has been trying to sleep. Although he arrives in an angry frame of mind, he is soon pacified by the party-goers and despite his intention to go straight back to bed, he is one of the last people to leave the house.

Keyword
Participate

Element
Air

Planet
Uranus ♅

DEGREE 20

Keyword
Concentration

Element
Air

Planet
Uranus ♅

Children out on a picnic do not appear to notice the flies and other insects which gather to enjoy the feast, nor are they bothered by the occasional chilly breeze that might upset adults present. Perhaps children are too busy enjoying themselves to pay attention to such trivialities.

DEGREE 21

The swan is a beautiful creature. Its grace of form and regal bearing set it apart from other birds. Beneath the saintly and pristine exterior, however, the story is very different. Swans are birds of volatile and aggressive temperament and have wings powerful enough to break a human arm.

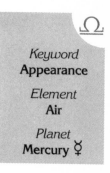

Keyword
Appearance

Element
Air

Planet
Mercury ☿

DEGREE 22

Keyword
Doubt

Element
Air

Planet
Mercury ☿

Lying in bed night after night, a child is terrified by the wardrobe which stands at the end of the bed. On the eve of her birthday, the child's mother puts her presents in the wardrobe. Once she has conquered her fear enough to retrieve the gifts, the child views the wardrobe with far less trepidation.

DEGREE 23

A fussy and awkward customer accuses a greengrocer of possessing scales that are set in his favour. When he proves conclusively that any aberration in the scales' accuracy is clearly in favour of the customer she is satisfied. However, she does not offer to pay for all the extra vegetables she has had at the greengrocer's expense for a number of years.

Keyword
Balance

Element
Air

Planet
Mercury ☿

DEGREE 24

Keyword
Compassion

Element
Air

Planet
Mercury ☿

A judge about to pass sentence on a criminal is aware, prior to the judgement, of the laughter of children who are playing outside in the street. The offender before him is not long out of childhood and the judge decides to give him another chance. He passes a suspended sentence.

DEGREE 25

Working all day with gold and precious stones, the jeweller designs and creates delicate and fashionable settings. His expertise is not in doubt but the craftsman could never afford to buy for himself any of the jewellery that he creates.

Keyword
Irony

Element
Air

Planet
Mercury ☿

DEGREE 26

♎

Keyword
Undertone

Element
Air

Planet
Mercury ☿

The windmill owes its efficiency not only to the great vanes that drive the grinding stones but also to the small vane or paddle at the back of the mill that keeps the windmill facing into the prevailing wind. Without this device the mill could only work on certain days.

DEGREE 27

Keyword
Continuity

Element
Air

Planet
Mercury ☿

Many great ships were once built and repaired in the now deserted dockyard. Most of the vessels are now only a memory, having been scrapped years before. Although the yard itself has not been in use for a very long time, so solidly was it built that it might well outlive the next generation of ships also.

DEGREE 28

♎

Keyword
Learning

Element
Air

Planet
Mercury ☿

Broken barrels in a brewery all find their way to the cooper, whose art goes back many hundreds of years. The tools he uses have not changed significantly in all that time, nor have the techniques involved. The skill lies not in the methods but in the precision which, like his ancestors, the cooper gained only by experience.

DEGREE 29

In the final of an important competition a golfer mislays his favourite putter. He blames losing the contest on the absence of the club in question, though the one he borrowed was of identical manufacture and weight.

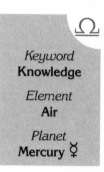

Keyword
Knowledge

Element
Air

Planet
Mercury ☿

Keyword
Periodical

Element
Air

Planet
Mercury ☿

DEGREE 30

An aged music hall entertainer who was once a household name is now rarely recognised in the street. For a brief period, songs and routines from his era come back into fashion and for a short while the entertainer is once again in demand. After the interlude he is cast back into his accustomed obscurity.

SCORPIO

♏

Darkest of dark, deepest of deep. The end marks a moment to begin and the very darkness appears as a cloak to mask the magician's deception. True magic is cloaked in light, known to all yet truly understood only by the enlightened perpetually ignorant.

Moon ☽	Sun ☉	Mercury ☿	Venus ♀	Mars ♂
Jupiter ♃	Saturn ♄	Uranus ♅	Neptune ♆	Pluto ♇

DEGREE 1

♏

The surgeon's hands are both his skill and his living, so he is dejected when they are damaged in an accident. As his bitterness passes, he finds himself teaching others his skills, and in so doing acquires a verbal dexterity that he never possessed before. Even when his hands eventually heal, he does not go back to his former existence.

Keyword
Circumstance

Element
Water

Planet
Mars ♂

♏

DEGREE 2

Keyword
Protection

Element
Water

Planet
Mars ♂

As anyone who touches a nettle, or worse still falls into a bed of them, knows to their cost, the sting of this plant can be both irritating and painful. The gardener who dons leather gloves, however, grasps and uproots the plants with immunity.

DEGREE 3

♏

In the closing stages of a marathon, a particular runner is forcing himself on with determination alone. Mile after weary mile he pushes his exhausted body forward. After the race he spends many days recovering mentally and physically from the self-imposed ordeal but considers the suffering to have been worthwhile. His finishing position was 23rd out of 30.

Keyword
Tenacity

Element
Water

Planet
Mars ♂

♏

DEGREE 4

Keyword
Opinion

Element
Water

Planet
Mars ♂

Alone and quiet in a padded cell, a woman branded as a lunatic because of a single mistake made early in life, considers her situation. Her recent violent outburst has only confirmed the opinion of her doctors that she is unstable, although the woman herself sees her actions as quite rational in view of the frustration she is forced to endure.

DEGREE 5

A lumberjack holds the record for the number of trees felled in a single month. He and his colleagues are well aware of the animosity felt towards them by conservationists who feel that the trees should be preserved. For the last 20 years, in his spare time, the lumberjack has been creating elegant and beautiful reproduction furniture.

Keyword
Multi-faceted

Element
Water

Planet
Mars ♂

DEGREE 6

Keyword
Perception

Element
Water

Planet
Mars ♂

A master of his craft, the knife grinder daily pushes his cart round the streets of a busy city and is always welcomed by the housewives, who value his skill. The knife sharpener is aware of his usefulness but does not return too quickly to the same district for he knows that he will be more welcome when knives are blunt.

DEGREE 7

An engineer designs and builds a steam locomotive more efficient and streamlined than any before. He is proud of his achievement as it rolls out of the station for the first time. Two hours later the locomotive is wrecked as a result of a faulty track that, in his love affair with his creation, the engineer has failed to have replaced.

♏

Keyword
Overview

Element
Water

Planet
Mars ♂

DEGREE 8

♏

Keyword
Prevention

Element
Water

Planet
Mars ♂

Almost everyone is apprehensive about the dentist, though in actual fact the majority of practitioners are gentle and rarely cause any discomfort to their patients. The greatest fear, however, is generated within those people who have not taken care of their teeth adequately and therefore spend the longest period sitting in the dentist's chair.

DEGREE 9

Calculated risks are part of the stuntsman's life. Every day he dives through windows or leaps from balconies. When asked by friends, who admire his skill and athletic ability, if he will accompany them on a rock climbing expedition, the stuntsman declines, declaring the pastime to be too dangerous.

Keyword
Limitation

Element
Water

Planet
Mars ♂

DEGREE 10

Keyword
Understanding

Element
Water

Planet
Mars ♂

Devastating all before it, a plague sweeps through Western Europe. A certain small village is affected and though the inhabitants know they could escape into the surrounding countryside, they are also aware that they may carry the infection with them. Unanimously they decide to close their village to the outside world until the plague has run its course amongst them.

DEGREE 11

In the back streets of a large city, an elderly barber carries on his trade. Because his technique is neither stylish nor modern, young people avoid his premises. One day, while passing a fashionable hair stylist's in an up-market part of town, he discovers that the styles he has maintained for years are now back in fashion, but at ten times the price he charges.

Keyword
Full circle

Element
Water

Planet
Neptune ♆

DEGREE 12

Keyword
Reality?

Element
Water

Planet
Neptune ♆

Deserted except for a few local children after a major event, a huge arena stands quiet. The children, ragged urchins from a shanty town close by, are playing at racing on the running track. One of the older children, unseen by cheering crowds and with no stop watch to monitor him, breaks several world records on the track.

DEGREE 13

Mightiest of the big cats, the tiger is a supreme hunter. Efficient and deadly, she stalks through the tangled jungle or over rolling plains. Yet for all her ferocity in the kill, and despite the tremendous power in her feet and claws, back in the lair with her cubs she is a responsive and gentle mother.

♏

Keyword
Variable

Element
Water

Planet
Neptune ♆

♏

Keyword
Utilisation

Element
Water

Planet
Neptune ♆

DEGREE 14

With little choice after arriving late at a battleground, a commander picks the bottom of the hill, having noticed the fallen snow and anticipating a rising wind. His opponent is jubilant and orders his archers to advance down the hill. Soon the wind blows snow into their faces and their arrows fall short. At the bottom of the hill, the opposing archers pick up the fallen arrows and fire

DEGREE 15

In folklore and legend, snakes have always been partly revered and partly hated. Often representing the Devil in Western countries, where it is not particularly prevalent, the snake has, in countries with a greater number of species, attracted a rather more regal status. Unknowing, the snake continues to slither about as it has done for hundreds of thousands of years.

Keyword
Perspective

Element
Water

Planet
Neptune ♆

♏

Keyword
Healing

Element
Water

Planet
Neptune ♆

DEGREE 16

Busy and a little flustered, a tired nurse stops to adjust the pillow of a patient. The person in the bed looks at the tired face and smiles. As the nurse surveys the trusting, grateful invalid, her exhaustion passes away and she continues her duties with a lightened step. Her compassion is her cure.

DEGREE 17

An excess of garlic in the diet is likely to lead, in certain countries at least, to social isolation, for the smell of garlic is pungent in the sweat and on the breath of those who consume it. Nevertheless, garlic cleans the stomach, purifies the blood and is virtually undetectable to an individual who has also eaten it.

Keyword
Alternate

Element
Water

Planet
Neptune ♆

DEGREE 18

Keyword
Present

Element
Water

Planet
Neptune ♆

At the scene of a road accident, a passer-by takes charge of the situation, dressing the wounds of the injured and saving the life of one. When the emergency services arrive the hero slips away quietly, unwilling to be recognised as a former doctor who was dismissed for unprofessional conduct years before.

DEGREE 19

A vixen out hunting steals from a flock containing two lambs, one of which is sickly. The shepherd gives chase and eventually the vixen drops the lamb. By the time the shepherd returns to the flock he discovers that the vixen has doubled back in his absence and taken the healthy lamb.

Keyword
Thought

Element
Water

Planet
Neptune ♆

DEGREE 20

Keyword
Resilience

Element
Water

Planet
Neptune ♆

The vineyard does not require particularly good soil. Vines will grow in the most difficult of places, provided they have sufficient heat and water. Growing where other crops might well fail, this remarkable plant is turned, with the help of humanity, into liquid sunshine.

DEGREE 21

For years a certain business executive has maintained an extremely hectic and stressful career, and is proud of his company's success. Eventually, through overwork, he falls ill for a lengthy period and is astonished to discover that the company survives without him.

Keyword
Importance?

Element
Water

Planet
Moon ☽

DEGREE 22

♏

Keyword
Appearance

Element
Water

Planet
Moon ☽

Strange and apparently horrific devices are laid out neatly in the sterile operating theatre. Though at first glance it has the appearance of an ultra clean torture chamber, the room offers new life to many who are brought within its confines.

DEGREE 23

Unobtrusive and retiring, the scorpion is a lover of dark corners and will rarely show itself. Silent to the world at large, the creature enjoys a hermit-like existence. However, should it be disturbed or cornered the creature has a vicious sting and courage to tackle adversaries many times its own size.

Keyword
Caution

Element
Water

Planet
Moon ☽

DEGREE 24

♏

Keyword
Command

Element
Water

Planet
Moon ☽

One night a policewoman with little strength or experience, is confronted whilst alone by a serious street fight. Although very much afraid, she orders the combatants to stop fighting. Such is their surprise at the sight of the diminutive lady and her commanding manner that the fighters cease brawling immediately and disperse in an orderly manner.

DEGREE 25

Elegant and proud is the old cockerel, who from his first herald of dawn, struts about, protecting the hens and guarding his domain. In this, his habitat, the cockerel is king, but like all the fowl in the run he could all too easily fall prey to a fox if he is not vigilant.

♏

Keyword
Caution

Element
Water

Planet
Moon ☽

♏

Keyword
Belief

Element
Water

Planet
Moon ☽

DEGREE 26

A veteran soldier spends his days relating tales of former glories to any passer-by who is willing to listen. In his own town his stories are well-known and generally disbelieved. Upon his death, amongst his possessions are found a number of medals. These, for the sake of modesty, the veteran never wore. Amongst them is a Victoria Cross.

DEGREE 27

Due to its ugliness and the generally unsavoury nature of its behaviour, the vulture must rank highly amongst the most hated of birds. Disliked or not, it is an essential part of the food chain, for in dealing quickly with carrion it helps to eliminate disease and filth.

♏

Keyword
Necessity

Element
Water

Planet
Moon ☽

♏

Keyword
Circumstance

Element
Water

Planet
Moon ☽

DEGREE 28

Any person who wanders too close to a tannery when the wind is in the wrong direction will certainly find the smell vile and offensive. If the same person were to walk into a saddler's or leather shop they would probably remark upon the distinctive and pleasant smell of new cured leather.

DEGREE 29

A locksmith is recruited to open a safe for which the combination has been lost. In a short time he gains entry to the safe. Noticing that inside it there is a considerable sum of money, he charges a larger fee than customary. The client for whom he has been working pays the fee and then enquires, genuinely, why the locksmith has never used his skills criminally?

♏︎

Keyword
Worth

Element
Water

Planet
Moon ☽

♏︎

Keyword
Presumption

Element
Water

Planet
Moon ☽

DEGREE 30

An unsightly scrap yard is visited by a pompous council official who asks the proprietor why he has not filled in certain documents which were sent to him. The scrap dealer explains that he cannot read or write. The official notices with some surprise the large and expensive motor vehicle outside, which obviously belongs to the illiterate scrap dealer.

SAGITTARIUS

Where does the man end and the animal begin, at what point is the liquid made solid? Draw an arrow of adventure, string a bow of enquiry and aim for the target of the moment. You cannot fail to find dead centre.

Moon ☽	Sun ☉	Mercury ☿	Venus ♀	Mars ♂
Jupiter ♃	Saturn ♄	Uranus ♅	Neptune ♆	Pluto ♇

DEGREE 1

Whilst resident in the embassy, an ambassador is considered, for all normal purposes, to be living on his own nation's soil. This diplomatic immunity also extends to the vehicle he travels in. In fact, despite the fact that he is an alien in a foreign land, he is often more privileged than the citizens of the state in which he is resident.

Keyword
Anomaly

Element
Fire

Planet
Jupiter ♃

Keyword
Trust

Element
Fire

Planet
Jupiter ♃

DEGREE 2

Feigning affluence, a young salesman in need of orders, spends his last few pounds on entertaining a potential client. He ensures that he is observed tipping liberally and generally sparing no expense. His ploy works and he secures a sizeable order, despite the fact that the client has seen through his pretence.

DEGREE 3

The emperor of a powerful state is in a quandary concerning a decision of national importance. His two main advisors disagree about the solution. In the end, the emperor takes the advice of the assistant who presses home his point in the most impartial and offhand manner, for the ruler considers that the cooler the individual, the more likely his advice is to be wise.

Keyword
Detached

Element
Fire

Planet
Jupiter ♃

Keyword
Appearance

Element
Fire

Planet
Jupiter ♃

DEGREE 4

A titled lady attends a tea party, held in the summer on the lawn of a large stately home. Although she discourses with rich and influential people for most of the afternoon, the conversation she enjoys the most is with a maid whom she herself had employed some years previously.

DEGREE 5

An archer participating in a contest has one arrow left, with which he can either clinch or lose the prize. His coach knows that the participant will not have kept the score for himself and decides not to inform him of the importance of this last arrow. Cool, unconcerned and detached, the archer aims true.

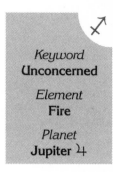

Keyword
Unconcerned

Element
Fire

Planet
Jupiter ♃

DEGREE 6

Keyword
Providence

Element
Fire

Planet
Jupiter ♃

Decked in finery, a recently ordained bishop prepares to officiate at his first important ceremony. He wishes to make a favourable impression. Just as he is about to depart he learns that the service has been cancelled due to a small but serious fire in the cathedral. The Bishop is not superstitious, but on a subsequent occasion he is less meticulous about his appearance.

DEGREE 7

Involved in a long and complicated court case, a barrister representing the accused finds himself becoming more personally involved in the case than he considers to be prudent. At a crucial stage he resigns the brief, believing this to be preferable to spoiling the defendant's chances through lack of objectivity.

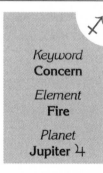

Keyword
Concern

Element
Fire

Planet
Jupiter ♃

DEGREE 8

Keyword
Appearance

Element
Fire

Planet
Jupiter ♃

An error in a column of figures is responsible for a misunderstanding of a particular company's financial situation. Trust is lost in the factory, which subsequently fails. During the winding up process the mistake is discovered but alas too late, for confidence in the company cannot be re-established at this late stage.

DEGREE 9

Faced with a hypochondriac patient who feels that she is seriously ill, the physician finds it impossible to convince her otherwise. In the end, the frustrated doctor prescribes a totally useless course of tablets and the patient leaves the surgery happy and already feeling better.

Keyword
Belief

Element
Fire

Planet
Jupiter ♃

DEGREE 10

Keyword
Innocence

Element
Fire

Planet
Jupiter ♃

The proud and majestic elephant can be trained, like many animals, to assist man in his work. The great beasts often perform their tasks with children sat astride their necks, encouraging the elephants by tickling them behind the ears. No amount of shouting or cruelty could achieve what these little children can.

DEGREE 11

In a particular city a powerful financier is approached to back a new scientific discovery that could prove to be of tremendous benefit to mankind as a whole but could also adversely affect many companies already trading in the same field. With an eye to the status quo, the financier refuses his assistance.

Keyword
Maintain?

Element
Fire

Planet
Mars ♂

DEGREE 12

Keyword
Providence

Element
Fire

Planet
Mars ♂

With honours even and everything dependent on the 18th hole, a professional golfer prepares to tee off for the last time in the match. Carefully he takes his stance, but as he swings, a bird flies across his line of vision, causing him to slice the drive. Though as a result he loses the match he does not mention the occurrence later at the presentation.

DEGREE 13

An illegal gaming house flourishes in a run-down and seedy property in the red-light district of a city. Those who play the tables are aware of the chances they take, but though they know that a police raid could take place at any time the possibility only heightens the excitement of their gambling.

Keyword
Chance

Element
Fire

Planet
Mars ♂

DEGREE 14

Keyword
Compassion

Element
Fire

Planet
Mars ♂

Whilst hunting deer, an experienced marksman sees a stag that he recognises in a forest clearing. On many occasions in the past he has tried to shoot the stag, but each time the wily animal caught wind of him at the last moment. The animal is now old and stately. The hunter chooses to leave it and search for other sport.

DEGREE 15

Spending a fair percentage of her working day on the telephone, a woman whose task is to sell insurance, repeats on each occasion the usual patter but rarely obtains a favourable response. Through insults and rebukes she remains impassive, deaf to all but the occasional positive reaction she achieves.

Keyword
Concentration

Element
Fire

Planet
Mars ♂

DEGREE 16

Keyword
Natural

Element
Fire

Planet
Mars ♂

The young ward of an elderly and seemingly uninterested businessman is surprised to find himself in the position of inheriting the old man's fortune in its entirety. The ward, never expecting a penny, always treated his benefactor without ceremony or reverence, an approach that others, not mentioned in the will, might have been prudent to emulate.

DEGREE 17

After a weary and hard fought case in a high court, a prisoner has been found guilty as charged. The weather during the proceedings has been very hot and everyone in the stuffy courtroom is overheated and exhausted. The judge calls for a lengthy adjournment before passing sentence, in order to cool off and review the case carefully and rationally.

Keyword
Wait

Element
Fire

Planet
Mars ♂

Keyword
Relative

Element
Fire

Planet
Mars ♂

DEGREE 18

Mounted on his favourite horse prior to the start of a race, a jockey who has performed well during the season waits for the starting gates to open. The time sitting in the starting stall, though only seconds, seems to him much longer than the duration of the race.

DEGREE 19

A millionaire asks for the bill, having eaten in a plush and exclusive restaurant. Calling the head waiter across, he quibbles over a minor error in the charge, which amounts to a few pence. The waiter immediately rectifies the bill in the customer's favour, assuming that the millionaire is likely to be correct. How else would he have achieved his present financial position?

Keyword
Belief?

Element
Fire

Planet
Mars ♂

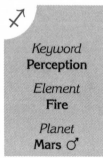

Keyword
Perception

Element
Fire

Planet
Mars ♂

DEGREE 20

Reviewing the work of two artists, a critic despises the work of one painter, who has many canvases on display, whilst praising the efforts of another, who has only one small sketch available for the exhibition. The critic is not entirely guided by artistic quality or style but partly by his eye to the future, for he is also a dealer.

DEGREE 21

With a host of successful seasons behind him, a footballer of international reputation retires from playing whilst still at the pinnacle of his career and immediately embarks upon a career in management. The player considers that a manager straight from success will inspire the same in others and he knows work will not be hard to find.

Keyword
Shrewdness

Element
Fire

Planet
Sun ☉

DEGREE 22

Keyword
Valuation

Element
Fire

Planet
Sun ☉

Dusting and polishing in a large house, a maid carelessly knocks over a valuable piece of porcelain, it falls to the floor and shatters into a dozen fragments. She informs her employer of the accident but instead of being annoyed, the owner of the house pays the maid the value of the broken item. Now consciously more careful, the maid never breaks another item.

DEGREE 23

Wandering along the paths amidst the quiet glades of a huge garden, a privileged visitor, allowed to meander in a private domain, feels at ease. The owner of the garden has money, the visitor has none, but then the owner of the garden is so busy making money to run the house and keep the garden that he has no chance to stroll pensively.

Keyword
Respite

Element
Fire

Planet
Sun ☉

DEGREE 24

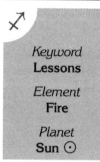

Keyword
Lessons

Element
Fire

Planet
Sun ☉

A professional darts player in the final of an international competition, requires only double top to win the championship. Poised to throw the dart, the competitor remembers the first game he ever played as a child and the thrill of realising his natural talent for the sport. His concentration lapses momentarily and yet his aim is true.

DEGREE 25

Certain inlets and ports on the continent of Antarctica are becoming blocked because of a build up of algae. This difficult to remove and productive life form caused no problems in earlier times because it was the main source of food for thousands of whales, which man has seen fit to hunt to the brink of extinction.

Keyword
Consequence

Element
Fire

Planet
Sun ☉

DEGREE 26

Keyword
Confinement

Element
Fire

Planet
Sun ☉

The political prisoner is freed from detention by a new political regime, though he is still advised not to express his radical opinions in the press. The dissident leaves his native land for he realises that he is just as much in prison in his own home as in the confines of the jail.

DEGREE 27

Jupiter is the largest of the planets in our solar system, though much of its huge surface is covered by poisonous gas. It is named after the King of the Gods, proving that though we may still have scientific doubts about its effect upon the Earth, the ancients had confidence in their own judgement, based on generations of observation.

Keyword
Scale

Element
Fire

Planet
Sun ☉

DEGREE 28

Keyword
Self-criticism

Element
Fire

Planet
Sun ☉

A social worker has doubts about her reasons for choosing her profession. She feels that she may have undertaken it to feed her own ego. Thousands of grateful individuals who have benefited from her advice and assistance could not care less about what has motivated her efforts.

DEGREE 29

With the Budget imminent, the Chancellor of the Exchequer has to please, if such were possible, all elements of society and yet still make the books balance. He may choose to hit one section of the community very hard instead of spreading the burden across the whole of society.

Keyword
Bias

Element
Fire

Planet
Sun ☉

DEGREE 30

Keyword
Observation

Element
Fire

Planet
Sun ☉

Having received a legacy, a young man has been extravagant in his lifestyle and squandered the money at his disposal. Though he does not regret having spent the money in the way he did, he is nevertheless aware that he could have used it to better ends.

CAPRICORN
♑

Rage and struggle all you will, for no matter how great the torment, the bonds that secure you will hold fast. Think the rope un-woven, consider the hemp not grown. Make the seed wither back into the mists of no time that ever was. Where is the scapegoat now? Behold, you are free.

Moon ☽	Sun ☉	Mercury ☿	Venus ♀	Mars ♂
Jupiter ♃	Saturn ♄	Uranus ♅	Neptune ♆	Pluto ♇

DEGREE 1

Standing upon the most elevated part of his property a farmer gazes at the vista below. From the hill he can observe, in a single sweeping glance, all the sheep and cattle contentedly grazing on the lush green pasture. He feels from this height that he could hold the whole farm in the palm of his hand and the effort of looking after it appears ridiculous.

Keyword
Perspective

Element
Earth

Planet
Saturn ♄

DEGREE 2

Keyword
Care

Element
Earth

Planet
Saturn ♄

With work scarce, a bricklayer is obliged to assist in the construction of a rather shoddy housing estate. The bricklayer is annoyed at having to build sub-standard houses, all the more so because he knows that one day work will be plentiful and these miserable dwellings will still exist.

DEGREE 3

Consider a recently bankrupted individual, who is suddenly in possession of a brilliant idea to make money. He cannot raise sufficient funds to commence his project because of his bankruptcy, but he could sell the plan to someone who does have sufficient money but few ideas.

Keyword
Option

Element
Earth

Planet
Saturn ♄

DEGREE 4

Keyword
View

Element
Earth

Planet
Saturn ♄

Because of the peace and quiet of his surroundings the man wielding the spade is very happy. His healthy outdoor life, free from restrictions and tedious routines, make this individual the epitome of contentment. Reflecting upon his luck he turns back to continue digging the grave that he has recently commenced.

DEGREE 5

Even their families would have difficulty telling the miners apart at the end of a shift, so black are their faces. Only when they emerge from the bath house do they once again appear to be the recognisable individuals that they really were all the time.

Keyword
Disguise

Element
Earth

Planet
Saturn ♄

DEGREE 6

♑

Keyword
Experience

Element
Earth

Planet
Saturn ♄

A trapped pot-holer has spent hours in the cold and damp of a cramped, dripping cave prior to rescuers reaching him. Despite the ordeal, a few weeks later he is once again exploring the twists and turns of the same musty cavern.

DEGREE 7

How can we believe in the passing of time as it is displayed by the hands of a clock? When we are employed in an enjoyable pastime the clock's hands seem to fly around, whilst if we are undertaking a tedious chore, the same hands hardly appear to move at all. All the same, both tasks will be over eventually.

Keyword
Reality

Element
Earth

Planet
Saturn ♄

DEGREE 8

♑

Keyword
Awareness

Element
Earth

Planet
Saturn ♄

An elderly lady is observed to have become apparently bored by social contacts and disinterested in company. A routine medical examination by chance discovers that she has developed a hearing defect. The hearing aid with which she is fitted restores her interest in the conversation around her.

DEGREE 9

Many men have been labouring for days, digging in terrain where normal machinery cannot be used. After some time a specialised excavator is delivered and manages in a few short hours to remove more earth than the men have been able to do in a week or more.

Keyword
Specialisation

Element
Earth

Planet
Saturn ♄

DEGREE 10

Keyword
Classify

Element
Earth

Planet
Saturn ♄

Who is the better man: the miser, who through pettiness and meanness spends a lifetime building up a huge fortune, or his only relative, a cheerful but none too careful man who squanders the entire fortune within weeks of the miser's demise?

DEGREE 11

Goats are adaptable enough to survive on just about any sort of food. In the wild they prefer mountainous regions and are invariably timid when faced by man. Their greatest advantage is their ability to utilise the most unlikely foothold in their quest for the summit.

Keyword
Adaptability

Element
Earth

Planet
Venus ♀

DEGREE 12

Keyword
Persistent

Element
Earth

Planet
Venus ♀

A trainee complains that the brick hod he is obliged to carry is too heavy for him to move around quickly and asks for a smaller receptacle. His employer refuses, knowing that doing things the hardest way at first can condition the individual more quickly in the long run.

DEGREE 13

Feeling his house to be too cold and his heating bills too large, a householder purchases a wood-burning stove. So busy is he, henceforth, finding and chopping wood, that he barely has time to feel the benefit of the fire. The exercise helps to keep him warm as well as fit.

Keyword
Ingenuity

Element
Earth

Planet
Venus ♀

DEGREE 14

Keyword
Ownership

Element
Earth

Planet
Venus ♀

A husband is convinced that his wife is involved in a clandestine love affair and as a result makes her life a constant misery by checking on her movements and accusing her of infidelity. After several years, his irrational behaviour drives her to the very practice he has always thought her to be guilty of.

DEGREE 15

If a length of rope breaks and is repaired by a correctly tied knot, it is a fact that the rope becomes stronger at the knot than anywhere else on its length, despite this having been the site of the rope's failure.

Keyword
Repair

Element
Earth

Planet
Venus ♀

DEGREE 16

Keyword
Mindfulness

Element
Earth

Planet
Venus ♀

Having been employed for general fetching and carrying duties, a labourer constantly advises his employer about effort saving devises that would make the job simpler. Eventually the employer dismisses his employee, buys the devices and does the fetching and carrying himself.

DEGREE 17

As a paid soldier, a mercenary is not obliged to believe in the cause for which he fights. To him killing is a lucrative job of work and nothing more. However, a soldier from the opposing faction who received a bullet wound would not stop to question the moral convictions of the man firing the bullet.

Keyword
Conviction

Element
Earth

Planet
Venus ♀

DEGREE 18

Keyword
Conception

Element
Earth

Planet
Venus ♀

Medieval stone masons employed on a magnificent edifice such as Canterbury Cathedral must have known that they would live and die never seeing the completed building upon which they laboured. It is possible that their satisfaction was achieved in small sections skilfully completed, which would one day be appreciated as a part of the whole.

DEGREE 19

Believing a somewhat dilapidated terrace of houses to be an eyesore, a local council clears the site and builds high-rise flats. The new flats are expensive and generally unpopular, losing money for the council. Meanwhile, terraces such as the one that has been destroyed become fashionable and worthy of renovation.

Keyword
Consideration

Element
Earth

Planet
Venus ♀

DEGREE 20

Keyword
Responsible

Element
Earth

Planet
Venus ♀

Sitting on the corner of a busy street a beggar rattles at passers-by the small tin that he holds in his hand. Some individuals put pennies in the tin, others ignore the beggar. A few even cross the street to avoid him, not realising that he cannot observe and admonish their meanness because he is blind.

DEGREE 21

Within his lonely cell a prisoner plots his escape in detail, his plans being the result of months of painstaking consideration. At last, within two days of his possible parole, the prisoner puts his plan into action but is quickly apprehended. With no chance now of parole, the prisoner starts planning again.

Keyword
Opportunist

Element
Earth

Planet
Mercury ☿

Keyword
Co-operation

Element
Earth

Planet
Mercury ☿

DEGREE 22

A stranger visiting a wheelwright's shop might have difficulty in understanding the hotchpotch of different parts that combine to create one cart wheel. No matter how well all the pieces fit, and no matter how accurately they are made, only the rim, created by a blacksmith and not the wheelwright, will finally hold all the pieces together.

DEGREE 23

The park attendant spends many hours in the autumn sweeping up the leaves that nature spills all over the lawns and paths. If he abandons his task before removing the piles of leaves, he should not be surprised to discover on his return that the wind has undone all his good work.

Keyword
Completion

Element
Earth

Planet
Mercury ☿

Keyword
Unorthodox

Element
Earth

Planet
Mercury ☿

DEGREE 24

A parish priest, bored with the generally accepted topics for sermons, instead commences to tell his parishioners about his favourite pastime, gardening. He is surprised to find that the following week his dwindling flock has swollen to twice its usual size.

DEGREE 25

The prime minister of a country approaches his nation's economic difficulties with pessimism and worry. Eventually he accedes to the pressures and is forced to retire. His replacement is a naturally cheerful individual whose attitude does much to foster a greater feeling of hope in the country as a whole.

Keyword
Attitude

Element
Earth

Planet
Mercury ☿

DEGREE 26

Keyword
Meaningful

Element
Earth

Planet
Mercury ☿

Travellers call to visit a hermit living in a draughty cave by the side of a road. Despite his pitiful poverty, the visitors are somewhat surprised to find him to be a cheerful man. Concerning his isolation, he is convinced that rare spontaneous contact with others is more meaningful than a constant babble.

DEGREE 27

Hold an acorn in your hand. This diminutive seed may be destined to give rise to a mighty oak tree which could, with the passing of time, become a huge forest. Each tree in the forest would be directly traceable to that first acorn. Do you not hold a forest in your hand?

Keyword
Credible

Element
Earth

Planet
Mercury ☿

DEGREE 28

Keyword
Deliverance?

Element
Earth

Planet
Mercury ☿

Having been born of peasant stock and lived all her life in humble serfdom, a hard-working woman is, by a change in the law of her land, granted freedom from virtual slavery. Horrified, she immediately rushes to the lord of the manor in which she lives to enquire what crime she has committed to deserve such a dreadful punishment.

DEGREE 29

A group of tourists stand and observe a tragedy being re-enacted in an ancient Greek theatre. The visitors are not familiar with the language or even the culture that inspires the performance. Despite the intentions of the original author, the exaggerated gestures and unusual costumes of the actors eventually cause the onlookers to dissolve into fits of laughter.

Keyword
Understanding

Element
Earth

Planet
Mercury ☿

DEGREE 30

Keyword
Motive

Element
Earth

Planet
Mercury ☿

Ignoring the rise of technology, a farmer insists on ploughing his fields using a team of shire horses. The farmer does not act from sentiment alone. He knows that his horses do not damage the good earth in his fields and he is aware also that one day the oil for machinery will be exhausted.

AQUARIUS

The new age dawns as the Earth

precesses back into the future. The

maiden sees her tired reflection mirrored

in pools of water spilled from the vessels

she carries. The load is heavy and the

world believes this water to be precious.

Perhaps we should realise that we stand

at the edge of a vast and

bottomless lake.

Moon	Sun	Mercury	Venus	Mars
☽	☉	☿	♀	♂
Jupiter	Saturn	Uranus	Neptune	Pluto
♃	♄	♅	♆	♇

DEGREE 1

A captain adventurer has been weeks at sea, driven by gales and with no idea of the geographical position of his ship. Knowing full well that he and his crew will soon be in desperate need of fresh water, he nevertheless appears cheerful and confident. On the day the water casks run dry, land is sighted.

Keyword
Confidence

Element
Air

Planet
Uranus ♅

DEGREE 2

Keyword
Apprehension

Element
Air

Planet
Uranus ♅

Faced with having to repair a car of unfamiliar manufacture, a motor mechanic experiences difficulty. The basic principles of the machinery are the same as in any other car but the badges on the bonnet and the boot are unknown.

DEGREE 3

An antiques dealer comes across a piece of furniture that he is sure is a genuine and therefore valuable piece of craftsmanship. Despite his certainty regarding the authenticity of the article, he is loath to make a purchase as the price is only a fraction of what he would expect to pay.

Keyword
Hesitance

Element
Air

Planet
Uranus ♅

DEGREE 4

Keyword
Situation

Element
Air

Planet
Uranus ♅

The responsibility for the safety of possibly hundreds of people is always uppermost in the minds of aircraft pilots. Such individuals are invariably methodical and totally committed when on the flight deck but may well be untidy and unpredictable away from the controls.

DEGREE 5

Intent upon the destruction of a section of society which he sees as being corrupt, a terrorist plants a bomb in a building he knows is due to be used for a government meeting. Many of those injured and killed will be the very 'ordinary' people he purports to support.

Keyword
Confusion

Element
Air

Planet
Uranus ♅

DEGREE 6

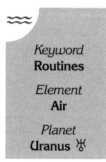

Keyword
Routines

Element
Air

Planet
Uranus ♅

Many clairvoyants have accurately predicted major world events but very few such gifted people spend much of their time considering these matters. The majority would rather assist individuals in their day-to-day lives and thereby shun notoriety.

DEGREE 7

A number of smallholders in the same locality each make their own purchases as regards their immediate agricultural needs. The time and money thus wasted is considerably reduced once they form a co-operative and buy their requisites in bulk.

Keyword
Co-operation

Element
Air

Planet
Uranus ♅

DEGREE 8

Keyword
Self-awareness

Element
Air

Planet
Uranus ♅

A commoner is present at a function otherwise frequented by peers of the realm. The fact that he carries no title leads the commoner to be rebuked by his fellow diners. He does not object in the least, for in this gathering he is unique and an original.

DEGREE 9

Devastating all before it, a cyclone weaves its path of destruction across fertile farmland. In its wake, people whose lives have been shattered in seconds endeavour to pick up the pieces and salvage what little they can. The rich feel the effect of the devastating wind more than the poor, for they have more to lose.

Keyword
Degree

Element
Air

Planet
Uranus ♅

DEGREE 10

Keyword
Habit

Element
Air

Planet
Uranus ♅

At the end of a lengthy and painful divorce case, the couple involved go for the first time, in the eyes of the world at least, their own separate ways. The marriage is now totally dissolved but a similarity in the former partners' mannerisms remains, evolved over the years that the marriage remained intact.

DEGREE 11

Busily connecting up dozens of wires according to their colour code, an electrician who has performed a similar task many times previously finds little difficulty. Any passer-by might be puzzled by a procedure that appears similar to sorting spaghetti, but then they would lack the electrician's experience.

Keyword
Learn

Element
Air

Planet
Mercury ☿

DEGREE 12

Keyword
Responsibility

Element
Air

Planet
Mercury ☿

A national leader who considers himself a pacifist finds himself in the difficult position of having to lead his country into an unavoidable war. Despite his beliefs, he does not resign, since he is aware that he is at least partly responsible for the deteriorating situation.

DEGREE 13

Should a child who learns in his late teens that he was born illegitimately consider his life to be ruined because of the discovery? Rather, if he must look back at all, should he not reflect upon the care and concern that has been heaped upon him as he was growing?

Keyword
Now

Element
Air

Planet
Mercury ☿

Keyword
Circumstance

Element
Air

Planet
Mercury ☿

DEGREE 14

A junior officer is court-martialled for instigating a mutiny amongst his men and is punished accordingly. Justice may be seen to be done, despite the fact that the young man in question took part in the uprising because of the unfair treatment meted out to his subordinates by senior officers.

DEGREE 15

It would be difficult for anyone not in possession of the facts to believe that a creature as ugly as a caterpillar could, in the fullness of time, be transformed into the beauty that is a butterfly.

Keyword
Metamorphosis

Element
Air

Planet
Mercury ☿

Keyword
Paradox

Element
Air

Planet
Mercury ☿

DEGREE 16

When a confidence trickster finds himself subjected to a similar deception to that which he himself practises daily, he is faced with a dilemma. He cannot seek the assistance of the police to try to recover money to which he had no right in the first place.

DEGREE 17

The duck-billed platypus is indeed possessed of a bill and, like a duck, reproduces by laying eggs. The creature is not a bird, and although it suckles its young, neither is it a mammal. For all its peculiarities the creature has flourished for tens of thousands of years, cocking a snook at orthodoxy.

Keyword
Difference

Element
Air

Planet
Mercury ☿

DEGREE 18

Keyword
Unexpected

Element
Air

Planet
Mercury ☿

An amateur radio operator picks up a distress signal generated half a world away. Because of his prompt action the crew of a large cargo vessel are saved from perishing with their stricken ship. The sailors will always be grateful to the attentive listener, whose hobby has been the means of their survival.

DEGREE 19

A satirical and cutting political journalist decides to take a more direct part in politics. Eventually he achieves a high rank in the governing party of his country and suddenly finds himself subjected to the same scathing criticism that he meted out to others years before.

Keyword
Return

Element
Air

Planet
Mercury ☿

DEGREE 20

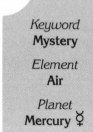

Keyword
Mystery

Element
Air

Planet
Mercury ☿

It is a fact that couples parted by war or national borders, who can see but not speak to each other, are quite capable of communicating telepathically. Such an ability eludes the understanding of science – and indeed there are many aspects of love that cannot be explained logically.

DEGREE 21

Aware of the vast distances between the stars that she or he studies every day, any astronomer knows that at least some of the points of light that filter in through the telescope may already have ceased to exist. Such is the time it takes for the light from distant stars the reach the Earth that the astronomer observes time as surely as she or he does distance.

≈≈≈

Keyword
Definition

Element
Air

Planet
Venus ♀

DEGREE 22

Keyword
Inner-knowledge

Element
Air

Planet
Venus ♀

By dressing and behaving in as unconventional a way as possible, we may consider that we are seeking individuality and a recognition of our uniqueness. If others copy our behaviour we no longer stand out from the crowd, but are we any the less individual?

DEGREE 23

Visitors to a zoo consider themselves to be viewing animals that are typical of their species. Nothing could be further from the truth. Only when in a natural habitat can any creature behave in the way that nature demands for its assured survival. The zoo is an artificial environment.

Keyword
Recognition

Element
Air

Planet
Venus ♀

DEGREE 24

Keyword
Attitude

Element
Air

Planet
Venus ♀

Strolling from street to street, the bedraggled and wretched tramp is shunned but at the same time pitied by most of the people who see her. Eating and sleeping where she can, she is content that her life should be as it is. Few people realise that she is living the life that she herself chooses.

DEGREE 25

The many theories concerning the force of magnetism remain just that – theories. Whatever the cause, pieces of magnetised metal cling to each other tightly. However, if placed with identical poles pointing together, instead of seeking to attract, the magnets actively repel what they erstwhile embraced.

Keyword
Opposites

Element
Air

Planet
Venus ♀

DEGREE 26

Keyword
Progression

Element
Air

Planet
Venus ♀

Human experience decrees that violent means must have violent ends. Extremists sometimes believe that moderation should be ignored and that violent behaviour can short-circuit the procedure towards meaningful change. All too often the only end achieved is a personal one of the extremists themselves.

DEGREE 27

Out on a coach excursion, a group of visitors are subject to a detour due to the closure of a road. They are at first somewhat annoyed at this change in their schedule but by the evening they are all forced to admit that the scenery they encountered because of the detour was some of the most picturesque they have ever enjoyed.

Keyword
Alteration

Element
Air

Planet
Venus ♀

DEGREE 28

Keyword
Forethought

Element
Air

Planet
Venus ♀

A racing driver, up amongst the leaders in a race, uses his intuition to conclude that the weather is about to change for the worse. He loses his position whilst in the pit having wet weather tyres fitted but soon regains it when the rain begins to fall heavily, leaving the other drivers unprepared.

DEGREE 29

Because of their understanding of planetary involvement in human affairs, astrologers are in a unique position to advise others on the best course of action to take in times of difficulty. It ought to follow that, possessed of such wisdom, astrologers themselves would never encounter problems in their own lives, but of course they do, frequently.

Keyword
Fallible

Element
Air

Planet
Venus ♀

Keyword
Endeavour

Element
Air

Planet
Venus ♀

DEGREE 30

Travelling over hazardous terrain, a group of polar explorers makes little headway. Such a permanently frozen and inhospitable wilderness will never be of any practical use to mankind and the laws of common sense would seem therefore to indicate that such an expedition is of no real benefit. The members of the party struggling towards the Pole would not agree.

PISCES

♓

The end is the beginning as the timeless wheel achieves full circle. All endeavour comes to this, motion without movement. Here and there a part of the whole appears stark and isolated, but within the blink of an eye comes to nothing and everything. At this stage, to the knowing, the purpose, no purpose becomes apparent.

Moon ☽	Sun ☉	Mercury ☿	Venus ♀	Mars ♂
Jupiter ♃	Saturn ♄	Uranus ♅	Neptune ♆	Pluto ♇

DEGREE 1

Returning home after an illicit weekend to a warm welcome from his wife and family, an adulterous husband feels pangs of remorse at his stupidity. It will take him many weeks to live down his feelings of guilt. For her part, his wife has guessed what has taken place and in her heart has already chosen to forgive her husband.

Keyword
Self-injury

Element
Water

Planet
Neptune ♆

DEGREE 2

Keyword
Condoning

Element
Water

Planet
Neptune ♆

Having assisted a burglar in several crimes, an accomplice, when brought to justice, is surprised to receive the same sentence as the man who actually committed the offences. The judge explains that since the burglar could not have taken the chances he did without a lookout, the accomplice who performed this task was equally guilty.

DEGREE 3

In his desperate struggle to obtain drugs, an addict is driven to acts which normally he would consider abhorrent and horrific. Despite his inability to justify these occurrences morally, he is swayed by his need for the drugs.

Keyword
Compulsion

Element
Water

Planet
Neptune ♆

DEGREE 4

Keyword
Search

Element
Water

Planet
Neptune ♆

Supported by a local dignitary to whom he owes his living, an alchemist spends many hours in his laboratory, seeking to create the philosopher's stone that turns base metals into gold. He will never find the elusive stone but he may make discoveries of other kinds on the way, albeit by accident.

DEGREE 5

Early each morning on most beaches, small groups of people can be seen, intently surveying the wealth of treasure left by the receding tide. Very rarely does the sea yield objects of any real financial worth, but just occasionally the beachcomber can expect the timeless ocean to yield a treasure of significant value.

Keyword
Occurrence

Element
Water

Planet
Neptune ♆

DEGREE 6

Keyword
Fantasy

Element
Water

Planet
Neptune ♆

Little activity is visible in the sleeper, whose only body movement is rapid fluttering of the eyelids. Subconsciously she is involved in adventures never fully experienced by the waking mind, for in addition to the running and swimming possible in everyday life, the dreamer can even fly.

DEGREE 7

So besotted is a young man with a woman he has met recently that, despite his knowledge of her previous wickedness and deceit, he is prepared to risk all for her sake. The immoderate love he feels renders him vulnerable because it numbs his common sense.

Keyword
Valuation

Element
Water

Planet
Neptune ♆

DEGREE 8

Keyword
Fault

Element
Water

Planet
Neptune ♆

A well-known medium is caught cheating at a seance by a psychic investigator and is immediately laid open to ridicule by the newspapers. There is no reason to believe that she has cheated before and many individuals swear by her powers despite the adverse publicity. On occasion she can still perform wonders, but nevertheless her reputation is gone.

DEGREE 9

Whilst travelling on holiday in the West Country, a motorist is advised that at a certain bridge he must stop and ask permission to cross of the fairies, who locals say own the bridge. The motorist laughs, for he does not believe in fairies. All the same, upon arriving at the bridge he takes the tale at face value and asks for permission.

Keyword
Precaution

Element
Water

Planet
Neptune ♆

Keyword
Consciousness

Element
Water

Planet
Neptune ♆

DEGREE 10

Under the effects of a hallucinogenic drug, a scientist partaking in an experiment is subject to a series of visions relating to his own research. The information received during a few short hours puts the scientist's endeavours forward by months.

DEGREE 11

In former times the existence of mermaids was never disputed by superstitious sailors who knew that the sight of such a creature as they put to sea was the certain harbinger of a shipwreck. Mermaids, they believed, were beautiful creatures to behold but must certainly be considered malevolent.

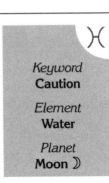

Keyword
Caution

Element
Water

Planet
Moon ☽

Keyword
Priority

Element
Water

Planet
Moon ☽

DEGREE 12

Being naive concerning the ways of the world, a farmer's son is tricked into parting with all his money in a gambling session. The money is the return from livestock so the youth is loath to return home without it. So long does he tarry that when he eventually returns home his parents are so pleased to discover he is safe and well that all thoughts of the money are banished from their minds.

DEGREE 13

When a nudist camp is opened at a certain holiday resort, the locals are at first outraged. Their protests are to no avail and in any case their attitudes soon alter. Quite apart from the money spent by the nudists themselves, much extra revenue is brought into the town by would-be sightseers.

Keyword
Possibilities

Element
Water

Planet
Moon ☽

DEGREE 14

Keyword
Understanding

Element
Water

Planet
Moon ☽

A Greek ruler is about to undertake a long journey in order to enlist the assistance of a famous oracle who he hopes will help him to sort out a governmental problem. Before he has a chance to depart, the monarch receives a messenger from the oracle laying out the answer to the difficulty, although the question has never actually being asked.

DEGREE 15

Continually subjected to false alarms, employees of a company are used to hearing the fire siren and eventually take no notice of it whatsoever. When a genuine fire breaks out, the management have great difficulty clearing the building, since no one believes the emergency to be real.

Keyword
Vigilance

Element
Water

Planet
Moon ☽

DEGREE 16

Keyword
Forethought

Element
Water

Planet
Moon ☽

In the heat of midsummer's day, the water of a picturesque canal looks cool and inviting. Passers-by are enticed to the water, for the sun's glare on its surface prevents them from seeing the jagged metal and broken glass beneath the surface.

DEGREE 17

A lone swimmer intends to cross a wide sea channel. He is aware of the distance but convinced that he can swim the number of miles involved. After further investigation he comes to realise that because of winds and tides, the distance will probably turn out to be twice that which is actually shown on the map.

♓

Keyword
Reality

Element
Water

Planet
Moon ☽

Keyword
Conjecture

Element
Water

Planet
Moon ☽

DEGREE 18

When a novelist undertakes a work depicting the future, unless he is possessed of clairvoyant powers, his vision of that future can only be based on a combination of present understanding and supposition. Much of his book may prove to be inaccurate, since human beings do not always act in a logical manner and nature itself can throw up some surprising twists.

DEGREE 19

A person who distills alcohol in a state where this is a serious offence could face heavy penalties for his illicit trade. He risks the wrath of the law because of the high profits to be made from a commodity that none is allowed, yet which all appear to want.

Keyword
Desire

Element
Water

Planet
Moon ☽

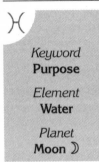

Keyword
Purpose

Element
Water

Planet
Moon ☽

DEGREE 20

Having spent a lifetime in study and self-denial, a revered guru is well aware that possibly less than one per cent of his students will ever achieve the spiritual awareness that he claims to be attainable. He knows that all his students will benefit in some way, however, and in any case, one per cent of one per cent achieving enlightenment will make his teaching worthwhile.

DEGREE 21

A prospective headmistress has job offers at two schools, one well disciplined and the other chaotic. She considers carefully. In the end she chooses the post in the badly run school since she reasons that anarchy may form a good basis for lasting stability if she can achieve the respect and goodwill of the pupils.

Keyword
Choice

Element
Water

Planet
Mars ♂

DEGREE 22

Keyword
Realisation

Element
Water

Planet
Mars ♂

A fabulously rich potentate spends much of his early life exploring debauchery, vice and low living. Becoming bored, he eventually turns to a totally ascetic life of self-imposed deprivation. Settling into his later years he finally manages to achieve the middle path that he now knows to be true wisdom.

DEGREE 23

An alcoholic is capable of using to destroy herself a commodity which is not in itself evil, since, like all things natural, alcohol is a gift from God. It is not the liquor that imprisons the unfortunate individual but her immoderate use of the substance.

Keyword
Moderation

Element
Water

Planet
Mars ♂

DEGREE 24

Keyword
Unapproachable

Element
Water

Planet
Mars ♂

Judging by the surviving statues in museums, the priestesses of the cult of Vesta in ancient Rome were often incredibly beautiful. Indeed they were chosen for the office partly because of their looks. All worshippers could admire the vestal virgins but none was allowed to touch women, who must have seemed as remote as their cold marble statues do today.

DEGREE 25

Wild ducks are extremely cautious, especially of man, whom they recognise as a natural enemy. Despite their reserve, if they observe even badly made decoys floating on the edge of a lake or stream, they will invariably land. The ducks' desire to flock overcomes their fear even of the voracious hunter, man.

Keyword
Instinct

Element
Water

Planet
Mars ♂

DEGREE 26

Keyword
Normality

Element
Water

Planet
Mars ♂

Looking out from the inside of their aquariums, fish survey the creatures beyond the extent of their watery world. Every so often these same creatures distribute food on the water or clean the sides and the bottom of the tank. Since the fish were all born in the aquarium, these strange occurrences are simply an accepted part of their daily life.

DEGREE 27

Far out to sea a fishing boat struggles against the prevailing wind and tide. The ferocity of such weather would prove alarming to anyone unused to the sea, but the storm-tossed fishermen sit below deck joking and playing cards.

Keyword
Experience

Element
Water

Planet
Mars ♂

DEGREE 28

Keyword
Time

Element
Water

Planet
Mars ♂

On the windswept deck of an ocean-based oil rig, men struggle with machinery cold enough to burn the skin from their chilled fingers. Far below them the thick black oil lies waiting, a remnant of the days when this place was a verdant tropical paradise.

DEGREE 29

Ignoring the niceties of civilised warfare, a general instructs his army to attack the camp of his enemy on the night prior to an intended battle. So surprised are his foe that they surrender with little bloodshed. By his actions the general may have saved thousands of lives, yet, even by his fellow officers, he is branded a coward and a cheat.

Keyword
Appearance

Element
Water

Planet
Mars ♂

DEGREE 30

Keyword
Return

Element
Water

Planet
Mars ♂

Far out in the unchartable depths of space a small sphere of rock spins in its orbit. This rock is not distinctive; in fact it is quite ordinary, and yet to the creatures that cling tenaciously to its surface it is everything. The highest life form that peoples the planet is on the verge of interstellar space flight, but no matter where they travel, this grain of sand will always be their home.

The Planets

SUN

The Sun is fiery, hot and combative. Oracle responses bound to the Sun by sign or degree must always be viewed in the most dynamic aspect of their interpretation. The Sun is the natural ruler of Leo, the sign of the lion, and wherever the Sun's influence falls, even in other Zodiac signs, some of the happy, fearless quality of the lion is present.

Whatever the answer you receive, there will be a desire for practicality in your approach to the response, though it should also be borne in mind that the Sun, through Leo, is ruler of the heart. The result means a degree of emotional consideration that one would more commonly associate with the Moon. Here there may be a difficulty: whether to respond solely with the head or to accept the more subtle messages that come from the heart.

Read the response again but this time leave discrimination behind, stand aside from the answer and allow it to filter through at its own pace.

Once you have assimilated the information that you have called through your own needs from the Oracle, and have accepted its truth with your heart, then you can begin to put it into practice with your head, exemplifying the middle path that stands at the centre of so many religions and philosophies.

MOON

))

The Moon represents one of the least understandable spheres of influence within astrology, hardly surprising when the phases and complicated motions of our nearest neighbour in space are considered.

The Moon rules all emotional reactions, so it can be expected to show up if you are looking for the answer to a problem or situation which speaks more of your inner being than it owes to the world at large. The Moon rules the stomach, hence the 'gut reaction' that is so symptomatic of the seeker's reaction to the lunar presence. It is highly likely that any other form of action will feel inappropriate, either with regard to the initial question or to the response you have drawn.

But beware, the Moon twists and turns, waxes and wanes, and rarely elicits the same reaction two days running. Perhaps it would be sensible to sit on your enquiry for a few days, if such is possible. Once you have done so, return to the Oracle. The response might be very similar, though you may not be as receptive to the capricious and inconstant Moon as you possibly are at present.

MERCURY
☿

Little Mercury, fastest of all the planets, is quickest to bring an instant decision, but this is not always the right one in the long term.

No planetary influence is either good or bad; all are neutral and everything depends entirely on the way that subtle vibrations are received and utilised. Never is this more true than with Mercury. Though the Oracle can assist you in your quest it cannot live your life for you. In the end the answers are yours to understand.

Mercury is quicksilver, liquid metal, a lightning quick response that will, on occasions, show brilliance in its subtle understanding of the erstwhile unfathomable mysteries of life. With Mercury present, the intellect is vitally important to your understanding of the Oracle's advice. Emotional responses are less likely to be of assistance in this case than they would be with the Moon in attendance.

Look for a flash, an instance, an unquenchable spark that you are quite certain represents your answer. In all probability this burst of inspiration is your immediate reaction to the Oracle's advice. If so, look no further. If not, re-phrase your question and look again.

VENUS

♀

Venus is cool and haughty but beautiful, and often quite specific. Still, there is a mystery that leaves the enquirer puzzled for some time and the process is more one of steady filtering than instant understanding.

Venus is the fountain of creativity, so it will hardly be surprising if you discover that there is a certain amount of work to be done in the building of the solution that eventually becomes clear to you. But it will not be toil of the hammer or the pick; rather, more subtle and steady remodelling that shapes and contours aspects of your life far beyond the apparent limits of your original question.

Patience is endemic here – not only necessary but also readily available – even to the individual who normally would possess none. The Oracle has spoken, so whether you are instantly in possession of the solution you desire or not, to look again would undoubtedly bring you back either to Venus or to one of its cool and calculating companions in space.

Do you accept the response of the Oracle? If not, there is every possibility that you have failed to understand what, in your subconscious depths, you already know only too well.

MARS

Red, brooding, hot and decisive. So the ancients saw the planet Mars. Rarely will you have to search deeply, either within the words or inside yourself, to make sense of the Oracle's responses that fall under the influence of the most immediate and positive planet in space.

But are you guided to Mars because positivity is what you genuinely need, or merely because it is so much a part of your basic nature that you cannot envision any other way of approaching your problem? Only you can decide.

There is nothing at all wrong with being positive and decisive; indeed these traits are one of evolution's most useful bequests to any creature. Sensitivity does not preclude the right or ability to make instant decisions, or to stick to them. Only be certain that your actions do not take you further than the confines of your immediate requirements, for prolonged use of force for its own sake can only lead to karmic retribution.

Mars is the ruler of deep Scorpio, in addition to the more superficial and fiery sign of Aries; either can show through in the various degrees that are ruled or sub-ruled by Mars. This may go some way towards explaining the duality that can be seen in the responses under Mars's rulership.

Even though you know that you have to adopt a particular path, you could well discover that your decisions are not as popular with others as you might have hoped.

JUPITER

4

Largest of the planets and known to the ancients as the King of the Gods, the overall importance of Jupiter to the stability and wellbeing of the solar system is only now becoming clear. Jupiter is expansive and joyful; it can lead you to your desired answers as much through an innate sense of happiness as through any deep sifting of your mental processes.

Jupiter is very large, as the overview you take of the various responses that fall within its influence may also have to be. The longer you consider them, the more far-reaching their implications will become. You may feel as if you are following the twists and turns of a long, long corridor, and the answer to the simplest request could well lead you to a much more fundamental understanding of your own actions and nature.

Although you must take all the responses of the Oracle seriously, there is often an element of humour involved where Jupiter is present. Riddles abound and there is invariably more than one way to see truth or a complex intermixing of truths apparent within the Oracle's advice.

Be generous with the world and in return it will bestow its riches upon you, no matter how perplexed or troubled you may feel yourself to be at this moment. The fact that you are led, or lead yourself, to Jupiter could mean that your problem is almost solved.

SATURN

♄

Saturn has come down to us in many guises, though probably the best known to modern-day man is that of Old Father Time. Astrologers from many civilisations have equated the ringed planet with the passing of time. The main inference here is that you will have to give your answer time to mature, not only in your mind but also in reality. Saturn rules Capricorn, the sign of the goat, an animal that always achieves its objective, no matter how difficult the obstacles that are thrown in its path. So it is with your question, even if the answers you receive might not be too easy to understand right now.

Confidence may be lacking in your life at present but you do not lack the ability to look forward and build upon a foundation that appears to be little more than an illusion at present. Create the circumstances necessary to allow the answers you seek to mature and then the response that you have drawn from the Oracle will become ever more clear.

Saturn helps you to discover yourself and to grow into a new and more fulfilled life. But beware, there often isn't much humour around with Saturn, even from the Oracle. You will have to provide that for yourself.

URANUS

⛢

Uranus was not known to our distant ancestors, only having been discovered in the 18th century, so it isn't surprising that its rulership is geared towards new thought, technology and the like. Revolutions can take place under the auspices of Uranus and that is why so many of the responses that it suggests in the Oracle demand a very radical form of action.

Uranus rules the 11th sign of the Zodiac, Aquarius, though it is reflected in other air signs. Aquarius is the age that the world is now entering, a time when convention is over-thrown and a breeze of fresh, new thought blows through many spheres of man's existence on the Earth.

The answer that you seek is no less revolutionary in its implications, even if it takes a while for you to understand how to go about turning your world upside down. Don't run away with the idea that all your preconceptions will have to be abandoned, however, for no matter how radical the necessary changes might be, they will filter through slowly and steadily. Sometimes you may not recognise that anything has happened at all.

NEPTUNE

♆

Most remote of all the solar system's planets but tiny Pluto, Neptune is the ruler of all mystical and psychic experiences. This means that the planet has a special place in the Oracle, which itself relies on the 'hidden' qualities of our minds to bring our own deepest realisations to the fore.

Elusive and nebulous, Neptune opens up new horizons for humanity. With this planet, the response you draw from the Oracle may be trying to convince you that you are asking the wrong question.

Read carefully, go away from the book and then read again. Coincidences abound in the vicinity of Neptune, and there is a possibility that exactly the same advice this book is offering will be forthcoming from entirely different directions.

Your intuition is the key, so avoid searching for an intellectual response if the Oracle guides you to a degree ruled by Neptune. Look inside yourself and hold the response in your mind without mulling it over. Very soon the lessons it offers will become abundantly clear.

The Elements

FIRE

First of the four elements, Fire represents the birth of the universe. Through it all things became possible.

All-consuming Fire, most destructive and yet most regenerative of the elements. The phoenix, when the time comes for it to die, is consumed on a funeral pyre which marks its demise and yet at the same time its rebirth.

Fire warms the cold but can also lay waste to the beautiful; it must be treated with the greatest respect. Zodiac signs that fall under the influence of the Fire element are bold, courageous, combative and persevering. That is the path that you must consider now, though there are many ways to display these qualities and not all of them mean making a loud noise or bulldozing your way through problems. Sometimes fire can burn cool!

Sooner or later, though, action will be needed; you cannot expect your present difficulties to be rectified without your becoming directly involved in the situation yourself. With a little confidence there is nothing you cannot achieve.

The fire may be in your own heart – the all-consuming, unquenchable sort that is not obvious to the world at large but can be very destructive to you personally. If so, the truths that you draw from the Oracle will show you how to balance the elements in yourself, find your own peace and bring calm to all those you meet.

EARTH

The good Earth brings forth, in its own time, everything that nourishes and brightens the world. Without the Earth nothing can grow, for through its antecedence nature passes from the sterility of fire to the nutrition that all living things require.

Your spirit lives, every bit as much as does your body, and in its own way also requires the solid dependable quality that is the Earth element.

The Earth moves slowly, waiting for the appointed season, watching and listening. Through its support the humblest seedling can move a mighty boulder or tear up a solid concrete road. How? Because it has never been told that such an occurrence is impossible and because with patience anything can be achieved.

If you have already waited a long time for your hopes to become reality but are certain that what you seek is right and good, take heart from the Earth element. Soon, all you are looking for can come to pass. But remember, life is full of paradoxes and coincidences. Things will work out, though not necessarily in quite the way you have been expecting.

AIR

Have you ever looked at an eagle, wheeling and soaring high above some mountain peak and wondered at the sheer majesty of flight? It is air that fills out the bird's wings. Invisible but present, yielding yet all-powerful. Impossible to live without and yet enigmatic.

Air is the unfathomable, the apparent nothing from which even fire derives its sustenance. In astrological terms it is the intellect, and the Air signs buzz with the vibrancy that reflects the *prana* of Eastern mysticism. To you at this moment, Air represents the assurance that you have the intelligence and the knowledge to derive benefit from the responses of the Oracle.

Answers often come quickly and with startling clarity where Air is present. Air is the gentle breeze of spring and the thundering gale of winter, so its intensity must be monitored and channelled wisely. Its only inherent fault is to be impetuous and thus cause you to misread responses in your desire to turn the world upside down immediately.

Walk wisely and with dignity, do not fight the wind that blows into your face but lean on it, draw strength and wait to observe where it seeks to take you. Your present and future motivation is important, but not more so than your constancy and strength. All is balance.

WATER

From the sparkling, bubbling stream to the deep, rolling ocean, water in its many guises covers the majority of the surface of our planet. Your own body is mainly composed of water, and inside you water is altered and replenished, as it is everywhere.

Astrologically, Water represents your emotions and psychic potential, these qualities reflecting the vacillating nature of the element. It is hard to hold water and just as difficult to tie down a whim or intuitive response, yet a great percentage of your life is composed of precisely these feelings.

Of all the elements, Water is perhaps the most difficult to understand, and this is reflected in the responses that comprise the Cancer, Scorpio and Piscean sections of the Oracle. Your answers may come drifting ashore on a gentle swell or crashing in on a tidal wave of sudden realisation; nevertheless, the means required to put them into practice are flexibility and intuition, never brute force or fixed attitudes.

Love, most powerful of all emotions, is never far from the Water element, as difficult to capture as the substance itself and just as refreshing and vital to our wellbeing. Somewhere in your subconscious you will discover that in love, more than in any other human expression, the solutions you require can be discovered. Love is the principle that underpins all of creation and it has more power than even the watery depths from where it springs.

INDEX

Note: All keywords, elements and planets begin with a capital letter.